Authors –

Brian Jackson

CU01023872

Brian Jackson is the Director of Expedition Wise Ltd, a charity challenge company designing, setting up and leading both UK and overseas challenges for charities. His whole ethos is the personal development of others and he revels in getting people to achieve their wildest dreams and fulfil their potential, whether that be on a London to Paris cycle challenge or climbing Kilimanjaro. His company, Expedition Wise Ltd, has facilitated the raising of more than £4Million for charity since its set up in 2009.

Brian has led expeditions and challenges all over the world to 6 of the 7 continents, working as both a leader and medic and especially loves spending time in the mountains.

In his spare time, Brian attempts to keep fit by entering Sprint Triathlons and is an active member of his local church in Wrexham.

Nick Pengelly

Nick Pengelly leads The Community Church Wrexham with his wife Sue. He is a director of several charities that work both locally and overseas, including the Erlas Garden Project, Catch the Fire UK and Teams4U. Nick is also a director in the thriving online retail Seed company, JustSeed Ltd. The setting up and running of his own company has been a fulfilment of a long-held dream, not only to be a business owner but to have a place where people can be encouraged to fulfil their own dreams. The completion of this book is part of his desire to help people find out what they are made for and to live life to the full. His life is always busy with 5 children and continued attempts to grow a giant pumpkin!

ISBN: 9781784565329

Front Cover Photo – Team member Thomas Carrick approaching the main, North summit of Karbu Ri (White Peak) 6,010m, a first ascent led by Brian Jackson in the Himalayas on the Nepal/Tibet border in November 2016.

Copyright ©Brian Jackson 2016

Rear Cover Photo – View of South summit of Karbu Ri, taken from main summit. A first ascent led by Brian Jackson in the Himalayas on the Nepal/Tibet border in November 2016.

Copyright ©Brian Jackson 2016

Testimonials –

"I travelled to Tanzania to climb Kilimanjaro with one of the authors of this book – Brian Jackson. I, along with others raising money for the Manchester United Foundation, climbed to Uhuru Peak, the summit of Kilimanjaro, in October 2013. This fulfilled one of my dreams to climb the highest peak in Africa and the highest free-standing mountain in the world. This book is all about how to achieve your personal dreams, it is well written and an inspiration. A must read for all of those who wish to follow their dreams." *Bryan Robson OBE – Former England and Manchester United Football captain, current Global Ambassador for Manchester United FC.*

"As a mentor, I'm always encouraging people to push themselves and fulfil their potential. This book is a must have for anyone wishing to achieve their dreams. A first-rate book with a great blend of stories and practical action points. An excellent read." *Leon Taylor – Olympic Medallist, BBC Commentator, Author and Mentor.*

"This book is a revolutionary catalyst of hope and fulfilment. A practical and edifying resource which I believe will aid many, individually or collectively. This can be utilised in groups and will benefit all, with the practical steps and advice given to reflect. Personally, I see this as the new up and coming ALPHA course, teaching us to grow, develop and strengthen our desires to fulfil our wildest dreams." *Jojo Meadows - Agony Aunt, Columnist, and PR Executive.*

"Brian and Nick set out the practical ways everyone can achieve their dreams. This book makes you look at yourself a little harder and a little longer, helping you work out what is holding you back from reaching your personal goals. It is also a glorious read in mountaineering, describing some of the most beautiful peaks in the world. I have visited Nepal with Brian and know first-hand how his passion for the mountains and his determination to succeed helps pull you through the coldest, toughest moments on a climb." *Jane Kirby – Journalist for the Press Association*

"Brian and Nick are people I know. They have a passion for life and are not afraid to dream big dreams. Their book provides both inspiration and practical guidelines to spur us on to achieve ours." *Elfed Godding – National Director of Evangelical Alliance Wales*

"Every year at Christians Against Poverty, we help thousands achieve their 'impossible' dream of becoming debt free. Seeing them filled with hope, restored and able to go on to live a life they never thought they could is simply stunning. As you read this book, commit to take the practical steps it teaches, and you will discover that you can achieve some big dreams." *John Kirkby – Founder and International Director of the charity Christians Against Poverty*

"I have rock climbed, ice climbed and been on an expedition to the Himalayas with Brian. He has been a friend for more than twenty years and his desire to see people reach their potential is in his DNA. We all have dreams. But how often are they not realized, because we either do not have the know how to make them happen or the courage to step out into the unknown. In this book, you will not only find inspiration but practical steps to take, so that your dreams can become reality as Nick and Brian share their collective years of experience for us all to benefit from." *Gary Sloan - Associate Senior Minister Rising Brook Church and former UK Director for Operation Mobilisation*

"Brian has led a number of challenges for the charity Railway Children, helping so many of our supporters achieve their dreams. This is a fascinating and captivating read which tells the tale of how others have achieved their dreams as well as inspiring readers to do the same. It is a very practical guide that will enable anyone to achieve whatever they want to in life. A must-read book with the inside knowledge of what we can all do to accomplish the 'impossible'." *Katie Mason – Events Manager for the charity Railway Children*

Acknowledgements

Both the authors would like to thank their respective wives, Steph and Sue, for supporting them as they spent the time and effort to fulfil the dream of writing and publishing this book. Their patience and support were much appreciated.

A special thank you to all the people who have given their time to be interviewed and enriched the book with their life stories. They have inspired both of us to push on with fulfilling our own dreams.

Thank you to both Harriet Walker and Steph Jackson for proof reading this book and suggesting changes where necessary. It is surprising how you read what you expect to read rather than what is written on the page. They also spent time to break down any technical jargon used. If there is some technical jargon that remains, we can only apologise.

A final thankyou to Rhiannon Thomson for help with casting her creative eye over the general layout and look of the book.

Contents –

Chapter 1 - Unclimbed Mountains *(Brian Jackson)*

"Reach high, for stars lie hidden in you. Dream deep, for every dream precedes a goal." Rabindranath Tagore – knighted and devoted friend of Gandhi, winner of the Nobel Prize for Literature in 1913.

"Tent tea, tent tea".

It's 4am on Saturday 16th November 2013, -20°C (-4°F) and I am awoken from my stuttered sleeping pattern at Base Camp at 4,600m (15,092ft) with the call for morning tent tea. As I sit up, I brush the tent roof with my yak wool hat I am wearing and receive a very early morning ice shower as hundreds of tiny ice particles, formed by my overnight breathing, fall down the back of my neck – brrrr!

This is day 15 of our Unclimbed Himalayan Peak Expedition to climb Chhubohe, pronounced "Chub Chay" and other unclimbed peaks on the Chomochomo Danda range in the Lost Valleys of Nar-Phu. That name alone, "Lost Valleys of Nar-Phu" provides a sense of mystery and exciting exploration into the unknown without even the wonderful dream of climbing a previously unclimbed mountain. Our 15 days so far break down as follows: 2 days flying in from the UK on an overnight flight via Oman; 2 days in Kathmandu organising the permits, buying last minute items of personal kit, sorting out all group climbing kit, and some visiting of the local tourist sites; 3 days trekking along the Annapurna circuit, a complete contrast to the riot and chaos of Kathmandu, trekking through the majesty, grandeur and serenity of the mountains; 3 days trekking into the Lost Valleys area to Base Camp walking through an area of Nepal only recently opened to westerners and feeling as though you are walking not just in a lost valley but a lost time; 2 rest days; and 1 day of climbing to summit 2 new unnamed and unclimbed peaks. These are subsidiary peaks on the far northern end of the same ridge about 5km from our main goal, Chhubohe.

...........The steaming mug of tea is handed to me by Tendi Sherpa, one of the two climbing Sherpas we have with our team. The team consists of Bug Wrightson, a freelance outdoor activities leader, Ian Foster, an outdoor equipment retailer, and myself, Brian Jackson, a director of a charity challenge company called Expedition Wise.

I sip my tea whilst still lying inside my sleeping bag, reticent to struggle out of it into the icy cold of the tent, thinking of what lies ahead. We are attempting to be the first people in history to stand on the summit of a previously unclimbed mountain, Chhubohe, in the Nepalese Himalayas. A shiver of anticipation runs through my body – this is a 38 year old dream that could now become a reality. All the detailed planning, saving, accumulation of leave, and training could, within 10-12 hours, be realised.

I finish my tea and now begin the arduous task of warming my Spantik double boots which I have kept inside my sleeping bag overnight to stop them from freezing. It takes me almost an hour to dress myself in several layers of clothing, warm my boots enough to fit my feet, and check my harness, helmet, goggles, jumar and climbing kit. I then waddle in all my oversized down clothing to the mess tent to try and force down some breakfast porridge. I have never been great at eating early in the morning (or night) and with the excitement of what lies ahead, find it very hard to eat as much as I know I will need for the climb ahead. Our team of Bug, Pasang Sherpa, Tendi Sherpa and I set off for the South West face of Chhubohe. Ian is unfortunately suffering from a chest infection which has kept him up all night coughing, leaving him exhausted this morning, but he still braves the cold to eat breakfast with us before waving us off...........

Let me backtrack a bit if I may. One year previously, I had decided that the time was right to fulfil one of my longest held dreams and attempt to climb an unclimbed mountain in Nepal. I emailed the Nepalese Ministry of Culture, Tourism and Civil Aviation to ask for the latest list of newly opened unclimbed peaks. From this list of 103 peaks, I had selected one main peak in a region north of the Annapurna range in the romantically named "Lost Valleys of Nar Phu" – Chhubohe. There were two reasons for choosing Chhubohe. Firstly I had not been to the Annapurna region of Nepal and secondly and far more important, it was the lowest of all the peaks on the list at 5,603m (18,382ft), the height to be confirmed upon climbing it, which suited me just fine.

Knowing November to be a good month to trek in Nepal, I set the date for the climb as November 2013 and paid for the necessary climbing permit. Now all I had to do was earn the money for the actual challenge, arrange the in-country support, buy some more kit (never really a hardship), recruit some other fellow dreamers, sort out work so I could leave it running without me and convince Steph, my wife, that I could take the whole month of November off to chase a 38 year old dream.

I was 8 years old when I saw my first photograph of Tenzing Norgay and Edmund Hilary standing on the virgin summit of Everest. Upon seeing that photograph, I instantly knew that this is what I wanted to do, not to climb Everest as this had now been climbed, but to stand on the summit of a mountain that no one had ever climbed before. This dream was so clear to me at the age of 8 but it had taken me 38 years to reach this time now when I was sending out an e-mail to everyone I knew asking if they would like to join me in this dream adventure. I immediately had responses from Bug Wrightson and Ian Foster. Bug, I knew from his working with me on our London to Paris charity cycle rides. Ian I knew from countless 3 Peaks charity challenges and our "Old Man's Trip to Mount Elbrus" the previous year. The team was formed and the challenge set – we were off!

………we start walking at 5am on the frozen turf and slate and zigzag our way towards the South West face. I am feeling both confident and anxious in equal measure. Confident, as two days previously, Pasang Sherpa and I have already climbed 2 previously unclimbed and

unnamed subsidiary peaks on the Chomochomo Danda range at 5,506m (18,064ft) and 5,610m (18,405ft) respectively. We named them "Dada" which means Hill and "Kaloche" meaning Black Peak, named after Arnold Black, a friend of mine who had recently lost his battle with Pancreatic Cancer. I am therefore quietly confident I can climb to this height and that I will not get suffer with any high altitude sickness on route. I am also however extremely anxious as I know the snow conditions are appalling with deep non-formed sugar crystals. I also have the very real worry that the single day of rest between climbing the subsidiary peaks and attempting this longer, harder climb may not have given me enough time to recover and that I may still yet fail in achieving my dream by having to turn around before the summit. With this not all together positive outlook playing in the back of my mind, I continue trudging on with the team, slightly out of breath on each step. As I periodically stop to get my breath back I realise I am overthinking things and worrying myself. At my next pause for more oxygen, I have a little chat with myself to just enjoy the climb and stop worrying. I actually mutter this out loud and the others must think I have possibly lost it but they politely ignore my ramblings. We take just over 2 hours to reach the South West Face proper and the snow line. The climb so far has been hard with both Bug and I struggling for breath in the extreme cold and the weight of carrying all of our climbing kit. The Sherpas of course are finding it very easy and are carrying all the fixed rope and snow stakes. We would certainly not be able to climb this mountain without them. We stop at the snow line to *prepare for moving as a team of 4 up onto the snow face. We pull all of our equipment from our rucksacks and in the light of our head torches, attempt to rope up together with fingers that refuse to work in large down mittens, so are forced to work with only our small inner gloves on. The material equipment is frozen rigid and fights against our efforts to mould it to the required shape to fit our bodies and the metallic kit is painful to touch even through our inner gloves. Eventually, after a lot of effort and very cold hands, we finish harnessing up, attaching our crampons, donning our helmets, and tying onto the rope as our team of 4, and now wield our ice axes as we start the actual climb.*

I think that maybe I was mistaken about the quality of the snow and need not have worried as the first 10 paces are solid with the reassuring crunch and great squeaking sound of solid compact snow. This is the sound that you want to hear, as if you are walking on blocks of polystyrene with just the right amount of give and firmness to each step. However, on step 11, I fall through the crust to my knees in complete powder and topple forward onto my face. It is almost comical but I then realise that it is going to be a long frustrating climb on the mountain face and will take all of my strength of will and determination to make it to the summit. We continue as a group of 4, kicking steps, each time breaking through the compact crust, falling through to the powder beneath and wading up to our waists, digging a furrow, sometimes resorting to swimming through the snow to slowly but surely increase our height up the south west face. I turn my mind off the pain and frustration of the poor snow conditions and just focus on moving forward however slowly, one step at a time; step, pause, breathe, move on, step, pause, breathe, move on…. Even when the slope kicks up to a steeper angle of 75°, the snow is still fighting us and causes us to slide backwards one step for every two we move forwards, frustrating us and sapping our energy in the cold dark morning. Climbing at altitude is so much more than just physical as it takes real mental drive to continue when you are hurting, the conditions are demoralising and it is dark and extremely cold.

Just as the mental battle is being lost to the exhausting and disheartening snow conditions, the sun crests the ridge above us on the face we are climbing and immediately we start to warm up. This lifts all our spirits and provides us with a burst of much needed energy. We stop to take a breath and watch as the sun floods light onto the Annapurna range behind us and we are privileged to have a front row seat to an extraordinary breath-taking display of every tint and shade of red, yellow and orange as the sun plays its rays across the mountains. We sit for a while until the sun does its work warming our bodies and reviving our spirits and providing us with the renewed mental drive that we need to continue. We turn back around to the face and continue up towards the ridge above us, now glistening in the sun. The sun's rays soon cause us to overheat in our layers of clothing but we are not really in a position to redress as we are now on the steepest section of the South West Face so we just sweat in our down jackets swimming through the deep powder snow with Pasang Sherpa leading the final steps to the ridge where we all collapse exhausted and extremely hot. The sun is so hot at this point that we strip down to bare skin to allow our sweat to dry before redressing in just one layer. It is the strange phenomenon of climbing in the Himalayas that you may well start climbing at temperatures of -25°C (-13°F) and below but when the sun comes up and reflects off the snow and if there is no wind, then you can be climbing in temperatures that reach in excess of +25°C (77°F), a crazy difference of 50°C (90°F) in the same day. We take on some much needed water and leaving our packs behind, take only the essentials for the final push along the South East Ridge to the rock summit of Chhubohe.

I really want to lead this section so that I can feel the reality of being the first person to place footsteps on virgin ground and also to get some film footage of the group climbing along the ridge with the Annapurna range behind them. I un-rope from the centre of the group and set off to break trail in the very deep snow. I place my ice axe in front of me, it sinks up to the adze, I then lift my right foot and kick 2 or 3 times in the same place to remove all the loose powder snow to create a firm foot placement, I then lift my left foot to do exactly the same with 2 or 3 kicks, I then move the axe forward and repeat and repeat and repeat. The rest of the team wait behind me for me to complete a section before moving up to me. This is thoroughly exhausting and I am soon breathing so heavily that the other 3 laugh as the amount of breath condensing around me gives the impression that I am a smoke *breathing dragon. I continue to the top of the ridge within 100m of the actual rock summit and then stop to film the team as they make their way up the ridge to join me. The views are awe inspiring and I feel so fortunate to be a part of this experience and see the amazing wonder of creation shouting out to me about the majesty of the creator. This is what I have dreamt about, walking where no one has walked before and experiencing the adventure of climbing on an previously unclimbed virgin mountain.*

The others join me on my perch on top of the ridge with only the final 100m to go along a narrow ridge of snow and rock with intimidating drops to either side leading to a pulpit of rock on the summit. This looks to be objectively more dangerous so I join back onto the rope and set off on the final section of the climb. The views to the drops on each side of the ridge are both beautiful and menacing which keeps my mind busy and the focus off the effort involved. We reach the final rock tower and carefully balance our way up it, our crampons scratching and gripping on the narrow 9 inch wide rock ridge. The ridge has a wedge of snow plastered to its side but after my first tentative step onto this, the whole snow slab starts to slip off the ridge and down the 1000ft drop to my left, I very quickly move back onto the rock itself. Just 6 feet from the top, we realise that the summit rock is actually two towers split by a 3 foot gap; "like Adam & Eve on Tryfan on steroids" says Bug. We have to jump this gap to reach the summit so we each take a deep breath, steel ourselves, and with the aid of the tensioned rope between us, leap over the abyss to land on our crampons on the rock pulpit.

Wahay!! Woohoo!! Amazing!!! We are all standing on top of Chhubohe, a first ascent in the Himalayas. I can't quite believe it and tears roll down my face as I allow the full emotional impact of my 38 year dream to fill my thoughts. I stand there quite stunned and need to take a quiet moment to appreciate what we have done. The others are all standing quietly immersed in their own thoughts until I whoop loudly and we start hugging each other and talking excitedly about where we are and what we have accomplished. We offer high fives to each other whilst taking care not to fall off the 3 foot square summit tower down the precipitous 1000 foot snow slope on the one side and the 1500 foot rock and ice cliff on the other. We check our 2 x GPS's and get readings of 5,640m (18,504ft) and 5,642m (18,510ft) so we plump for the lower of the two readings as the official height at 5,640m (18,504ft), satisfied that this is marginally higher than the original government estimate. After lots of photos in our charity t-shirts and banners, we take out our prayer flags and start tying them on between the summit tower and the ridge. We have now placed prayer flags 5kms apart on both the North and South main summits on this range of peaks and I am feeling a real mix of emotions - proud, honoured, humbled, excited, tired, complete, even relieved.

My 38-year dream has finally been realised. This is one of the most fulfilling feelings I have ever had. I feel I am completely in the right place at the right time and this is what I was made for. I have shared the experience with 3 fellow climbers who also shared the dream and I could not be more content or at ease with myself. This prompts me to ask what dreams are still on my list, what new dreams can I imagine? If I can achieve this dream, then I need to push on to fulfilling other dreams. I have set the benchmark and know I can achieve so this should now drive me forward to dream even bigger.

Hopefully this opening story has inspired you to think of the dreams you have or those you have had in the past. This book has been written to help you to fulfil your dreams by taking easy to follow steps, with the addition of other people's inspiring stories.

Think of your wildest dream, multiply by the biggest number you know and you can still never dream bigger than you can achieve.

Chapter 2 – "Unclimbed Mountains" Defined *(Nick Pengelly)*

It was while leading a 10-week course designed to help people identify and then pursue their dreams that this collaboration of two very different people began. I have always been passionate and motivated to help people find out who they are and then live out their dreams. During the course, both Brian and I listed as one of our dreams, a desire to write a book that would help people in this way. So the joint venture was born. We realised that by combining our different approaches to life we would be better able to provoke and inspire people from different walks of life. We hope that as you read this book you will be able to take the time and then focus on some of those things that are deep in your heart. We are not saying that the journey will always be easy, if it was I guess you would already have fitted your dreams into your life. Even writing this book has been a challenging process as part of me is determined and focused on the book, but a busy household and a number of other challenging times made progress much slower than I intended. Brian provided much of the necessary motivation to move towards completion. Some dreams will be easy and only require you to realise their importance to you, others will be more complicated, but by following through the suggestions in this book, I hope that they can go from being hidden in your heart to being out in the open. You can then formulate an action plan and hopefully your inner desires then become part of a rich tapestry of a fulfilled life. If you need help finding ways to practically live out your dreams, we have provided some different ideas in the last but one chapter.

I love to read Brian's story and get inspired at the thought of someone having such an adventure and travelling somewhere no-one has ever been before; it gets me dreaming and thinking about the possibilities in my own life. Just to be clear, I don't have the slightest desire to follow in his footsteps, even reading his story gives me vertigo. My dreams are very different and don't include heights or mountains.

If we are going to discover or rediscover our dreams and turn them into reality it is going to take time, effort and focus. I heard someone the other day say that it was one thing for people in the past to see the distant possibility of mobile phones, it was quite another to turn the distant possibility into a reality. It was a scientist and inventor called Nikola Tesla who was one of the first people to see the future possibilities. He is reported to have said,

"The practical applications of the revolutionary principles of wireless art have only just begun. What will be accomplished in the future baffles one's comprehension. It will soon be possible to transmit wireless messages around the world so simply that any individual can carry and operate his own apparatus."

There are many steps in between the vision and the reality. Tesla believed that the necessary technology would soon be developed. I suspect it took much longer than he realised. Imagine being one of those people who had seen the future possibilities of mobile phones. There was then a long process of research, development, trial and error. To go on this journey and get involved in the early stages of development you would have to have first seen the possibility and started along a pathway to the dream. To keep hold of this vision and follow through the process, the initial vision would need to be very important. It was not until 1973 that the first handheld mobile phone was produced by Motorola. This phone was a far cry from what we are used to now and was hardly mobile due to its weight (1.1kg/2.4lb) and size. Technology has developed extremely fast and few of us would have predicted the central place a phone would have in society within such a short period of time.

When we start to look at the possibilities and dreams in our own lives we first need to spend time to establish the things that are important to us. We need to separate out the stage of dreaming from the stage of mapping out the pathway.

I have the privilege of talking to many young people as they are beginning to discover their life plans. Many of them have a clear idea of the types of careers that they want to take. The dreams they have in their heart begin to take shape, they often spend hours researching the options available to them, discover what exam grades they need to get and look ahead to any required additional education. To turn their dream into a reality they need to discover if it is a realistic option for them, select the right subjects, get good teaching and above all work hard to achieve the necessary results. Most of the young people who do well in this process have at least one mentor, often a parent or parents who are helping them navigate the tricky waters   Even then there are the joys of success and the pains of not achieving their educational goals. It is a very challenging time for young people as they try and find their dreams and move towards them. If you are struggling to think of the dreams that are important to you it is a good exercise to think back to the things you dreamed of doing when you were younger.

Mark has been kind enough to share a little of his challenging journey to fulfil a lifelong dream of becoming an airline pilot. Here is his story:

"It began with a schoolboy's simple gaze up into the summer sky. A bright clear vault of blue but with a thin white line of vapour trail making its way across from horizon to horizon. My attention was not so much upon the overall scene, though glorious it most certainly was, but upon the object at the very tip of the contrail, a commercial airliner. On reflection, this is where my dream began, and as I began to imagine, I had no inkling of the many challenges that would ultimately accompany the pursuit of a professional flying career.

You, the reader, if you are an airline passenger, may be reassured to know that the training of professional pilots is particularly rigorous. Such rigour requires the use of expensive equipment and specialist personnel and consequently the financial costs are high. When I commenced, some twenty five years ago, my new bride and I struggled to find the necessary funds. At one point, we were the only newly married couple I had ever heard of, living in a tiny starter home whilst in ownership of their own light aircraft! Windfall payments, tax rebates and salaries were devoured by a long list of courses and ratings. A relative of my wife died and the few thousand she was bequeathed went straight-away to pay for an instrument qualification. Aware of the toll such expenditure was taking on our finances, our social life and potentially on our relationship, I began to question the direction my dream was taking me. Given the demanding nature of the profession and the high standards required of candidates, a fair degree of single-mindedness is necessary in order to succeed. Though my wife was very supportive of my ambition to fly professionally, I nevertheless deemed that the point had come for re-evaluation.

Coincidence is the word we use when we can't see behind the curtain, but I leave it to the reader to ultimately determine whether events of the kind I describe are happenstance. At this particular juncture in the course of my training, I needed the full set of study notes covering all the required topics for the ground examinations, including meteorology, aerodynamics, navigation, and many others. The full set comprised some twenty or so volumes, some of which ran into hundreds of pages in length and were yet another necessary expense. The money was not in our account, so I trawled through advertisements in the aviation press hoping to find inspiration. In one magazine I encountered a letter written to the editor by the father of an airline pilot who had recently been killed in a road traffic accident. The letter, though short, was quite moving and, significantly for my needs, a full set of study notes free for collection was on offer. The letter gave an address and a contact telephone number. I called the number, and on speaking to the father the enormity of the family's loss was all too evident. In the course of the conversation he spoke candidly about his son, his son's career and the final tragedy itself. A rare kind of conversation ensued and a palpable connection was made between us. Towards the end of our discussion I was able to share my own aviation aspirations and, almost apologetically, I asked about the notes. The father said he had been overwhelmed by the response, both by phone and by letter, and perhaps the best option was simply to put all the enquirers' names into the proverbial hat and draw one at random. That evening I offered up the grieving family, and my flying dream, in a simple prayer and I presumed to ask for the notes as confirmation of direction. My words were not particularly eloquent nor theological but were certainly earnest.

It was a week or so later when the father telephoned me with some news. He and his wife had discussed the situation, and of all the few hundred people who had made contact, for some reason my name had kept coming to his mind. Our conversation then turned to the matter of collection and he asked where I lived. Since we were residents of Sussex and the address was in the North of England I had expected the necessity of a long car journey, but this too was to be provided for. It transpired that his daughter, who was visiting her parents at that time, happened to live close-by in Sussex, and she had volunteered to transport the stack of notes to her home for my collection. Not only were my immediate needs provided for and my career choice confirmed but through our meeting friendships began, both with the father and the deceased's sister. The encounter with their grief helped to put my aspirations in proper perspective.

There have been many other "chance" events that have occurred throughout my flying career. The provision of a low cost house from a housing association during the cash-strapped training phase, and, in an industry which is notoriously difficult to enter, my first flying instructor job from the very school where I trained. Another and very different kind of provision came in the unlikely form of a simulator assessment during my transition from co-pilot to captain that duplicated a serious in-flight failure I was to encounter a few years later. This training was crucial experience in dealing with the technicalities of this specific major control malfunction, giving me vital capacity to manage the psychological aspect of a situation in which there was a real possibility that I, my crew and passengers might not survive. However, the real coincidence for me is that the more I pray the more such coincidences seem to occur."

Not as extreme a dream of becoming a commercial pilot, I dreamed for years of being a vet, I am not sure if it was the grades required or the realisation that animals bite that put me off but in the end I decided horticulture and plants were a more fitting option. I still like animals but my interest in plants and horticulture is much stronger and is now one of my main hobbies and I have even turned it into a small business. I am sure we can see that there is a well-trodden path presented to young people to try and turn their dream into reality. They are encouraged to dream, they are encouraged to discover the things that are important to them. I am sure many of us who are older can look back at that stage of life and even in some cases wistfully look back at what could have been. We realise that since then many other things have crowded in including the pressures and challenges of life. For a young person, there are also now so many external pressures that I did not have when I was a teenager growing up. The crowding in of other things and the pressures of life therefore relates to all ages, whether you are a teenager, middle aged or much older.

There may well be a list of things that have not worked out as we thought. This book is focused on stirring up the dreams, maybe for the first time or just uncovering what has been lost. It may be that the early dreams are fulfilled and we just do not have the time to spend to work out what is next. In this book we hope to help you shape your future. This involves finding time to take your eyes off the day to day for a while and looking beyond. It is going to take time but we believe that it is time well spent.

As a Christian, my faith has defined many of my values and my core identify. Even if you do not share my faith there are principles that are valuable that you can apply to your life. Lou Engle, a Christian speaker once said "God has a dream and wrapped your body around it."

I firmly believe that each of us has a core DNA and identify. The Bible says we are God's workmanship or fabric which has been woven together for good things that have been prepared for us. These words speak of our uniqueness. In the same way that our natural DNA works to produce our unique features and personalities, I believe we have an internal identity which needs to be expressed to enable us to fully enjoy life. The same Greek word used in the Bible for "identity" is the root to the word "poetry". Each of us is a piece of poetry waiting to be written, full of depth, consideration and interest. Someone commenting on this said every good piece of poetry will have been rewritten many times. It may be time to do some re-writing. As you read this book take time to start dreaming. If your life had no limitations, what would you include in your dreams, what adventures would you have?

Part of this process of identifying your dreams is a discovery of knowing who you are and who you want to become. There is a scripture that says that without vision people perish. Putting this another way if you do not have any dreams then your life will not be fulfilled.

When I refer to a dream I am not referring to those that happen when we sleep but I am speaking of an internal desire and energy that, when harnessed, can shape and determine the course we take in life. We will find that when we have identified these dreams and started to work them out, they will have an impact on all sorts of areas of our life. Part of making your dream your reality will involve changing aspects of day to day life. A simple example of this would be if one of your dreams is to travel, then paying off debt and future budgeting might be an important step to take to reach this goal. You cannot spend all your money on day to day items if you need to save it to travel the world.

As we will see later, an important step to dreaming is to remove the barriers and obstacles that will limit us. Children are again a great example. How many children dream of being a professional footballer? The dream at this stage is not connected to their ability to kick the ball but to their love of the game. I often listen to one of my children as he plays football in our front garden. He is always acting out his dream, he names himself after one of his favourite footballers and he makes sure he has his favourite team's kit (with the name of a star player on the back). The game goes on for hours and of course his favourite player scores all the goals and his team wins. If you talk to him he will talk about his dreams. Most will not fulfil this dream and become a top footballer, but some will. Those that do will have normally had their sights set when they were very young. The important thing for these children is they are dreaming and they are practicing. If we can be childlike in our approach it will help us to engage our dreams.

As we grow older, many of us will not dream because we only see the obstacles. Being too busy and discouragement in life can be two of the biggest blockers to embracing life's dreams. As a child I was often told to stop day dreaming. Many of us need to slow down enough and find some space and give ourselves time to daydream again. Children dream and don't see the obstacles; in their minds there is no secondary plan. An example might be that you dream of travelling. To fulfil your dream of travelling you might need to take an extended period off work or delay going to university or starting work. The truth is you will not entertain the dream because the obstacles are too big. It might be true that it is not possible or it may simply be something we need to plan ahead for to achieve. You may need to plan on a gap year before university and manage your parent's expectations of you. If at work, you may need to take your plan for a sabbatical to your bosses at work, they might say no, but they may also say yes. You have nothing to lose. At this point, what matters is that you dream. Leave the planning to a later stage.

Where we are today is an expression of some of the dreams in our hearts. It is also possible that you have reached where you are today not through planning but by chance. If life is not fulfilling, then the dream process that we are going to guide you through will help you make the necessary adjustments.

One hot topic that is regularly highlighted in the news today is being careful with your personal data so you are not subject to identity theft. Many people find themselves caught in one of these scams through an email, phone call or other method. I received one of these calls recently saying there was a problem with my computer; it seemed fine to me. I decided to entertain myself and pretended to follow some of his instructions over the telephone. It was easy to see how innocent people could be intimidated by this approach. I found it very sad that these people are devoting their time to try and get access to private information and then through this, to access people's computers and money. This sort of identity theft is very destructive and can be very expensive too. There is another sort of identity theft going on in today's busy society. It is normal everyday people finding life getting so busy and complicated that they have no space, time or energy to connect to the things that were important to them. It might even be the case that you have taken a promotion at work or started a new job that has resulted in a career with more money but is actually no more enjoyable and may be even less fulfilling. You may have started on a course of study that has naturally progressed from where you were but is not a correct fit. One of the driving forces of course is the promise of more money or a better life job balance but something that is full of promise but does not connect to your dreams might even end up limiting your life. It might be that the increasing number of responsibilities you have picked up in life mean there is no time for actually living life. I recognise that there are different seasons in life that involve making judgement calls. I am currently in a season where just keeping up with the different school runs feels like a full-time job. There are things that my wife and I would love to do but circumstances mean we cannot do them now, but even so, we are still now talking about when we can do them, we are still daring to dream. Don't allow your dreams to die even if they need to wait for a while. Do not let yourself be subject to an identity theft that is as significant as having your financial world compromised.

There are many other motivations to make changes in life, it might be frustration, boredom, trying to re-establish life after a relationship breakdown, trauma or bereavement. As we look at the different dream possibilities, harness the energy caused by dissatisfaction and use it to start the process of remoulding your life. If there is no motivation to make changes then it is unlikely to happen. It will not be the energy from other people, colleagues, parents or relatives that makes this possible. They may be able to mentor you and help you along the path, but to sustain change requires our own internal energy to be released. I saw a great example of this internal energy being released from a stores sales person when my daughter was recently purchasing a new camera. The sales person we spoke to was clearly someone who loved photography. When we asked him about different cameras and their strengths and weaknesses he did not give us answers from a script that he had been taught but he referred to each camera, clearly as someone who both owned and regularly used a camera. He gave us the positives and the limitations of each camera and I think he must have owned 6 very good cameras himself from his descriptions. His enthusiasm shone through, clearly demonstrating that this was not only his job, which was a great fit for him, but a hobby that he pursued and loved.

We will spend time looking at dreams in the next chapter but at this stage we want to highlight the difference between your dreams and goals. When you have established your dreams, or at least some of them, then the next stage we will work through is turning your dream into a plan with a number of goals along the way. This second stage is important as we often need to be deliberate if we are going to turn our dreams into reality.

In a recent dreams course that I was running, one person said they would love to visit a seal sanctuary and see the pups being born. It was clear that this dream had been a long term desire. It was during a discussion that this lady realised that she could take some steps towards making this dream happen possibly within the next year. As well as researching the costs, best time of year and all those practical things, she looked at how much money she could save each month towards the dream. It was so exciting to listen to this person's plan and the steps she had taken. Even these steps of turning a dream into reality was generating excitement and life. Many of the big dreams that we want to achieve in life require us to turn them into short term goals. Each one of those are important steps to reaching and then enjoying the final objective. One of the things that is important when we are running the dreams course is to encourage people to believe that anything is possible.

Dreaming is about going beyond what seems possible. This may, of course, happen in stages. A few years ago, I decided to use my horticultural interest to set up an online seed business with a friend. When I now look at our online business it is far beyond what I would have initially put down as a dream. The dream has grown with the business and if you ask me now what my dream is, I would say I want to double the turnover as well as help more people step towards their destiny and fulfil their life dreams. As with many businesses, the initial stages were slow and hard work before things really took off. Most of my family were involved at different points as we prepared orders for dispatch at the same time as everyone was waiting for their evening meal. Each year we reached our next goal. As we got close to one dream a new one emerged along with the goals and strategies to get to the next step.

Daniel's story illustrates how dreams emerge and develop as well as the longer-term drive and consistency that are often need to see them fulfilled. Daniel Weston has had the privilege of representing Wales in the increasing popular sport of running ultramarathons. He has completed 6 of these races which are up to 100km (62 miles) long. Daniel has managed to reach a high level even with its vigorous training regime while maintaining a full time job and busy family life. It is interesting to hear what motivates him and how his dream of being one of the top ultramarathon runners developed.

Daniel's example came from his Dad whom he admired; his Dad loved running and would win local races. As a child he saw his Dad as someone with superhuman power. They did some running together and his Dad would talk about running. His advice was always very simple and at times would have seemed blunt in its truthfulness, if you did not know how kind a man he is. On one occasion having finished a 5 mile run Daniel's Dad commented "It's simple, you just need to run quicker". Although Daniel enjoyed running, he had to prioritise his work and he did not return to running until he was 26 years old.

Daniel has now developed a very clear and practical approach to his training schedule. He said,

> **"Doing the impossible comes from doing what is possible today.** When I started, I would run 7.5 minute miles and running under 6 minute miles was impossible. I now do it every day."

He continued to explain how it needs a change of mind set to be able to achieve success.

> **"Before the possible you must do the necessary.** This base period involves very slow miles but if you don't do this necessary work over an extended period you will stress your body. Many people burn themselves out due to injury at this point rather than build in the injury prevention. The next stage is to start pushing a bit harder where there is a 40% possibility of not reaching your training target."

This consistent training regime for over 10 years has led to Daniel running at international level and times of 7 hours 11 minutes for 100km. When I was speaking to Daniel he was in the middle of another period of 'necessary training' as he prepared for his next 100km race. Daniel's dream was to run and after success at marathons he was looking for the next challenge which came in the form of an opportunity to run in an ultramarathon. He dreams now of improving his time in ultramarathons.

This story demonstrates many of the things we will need to do to fulfil dreams, particularly those that can only happen over time. Whether it is a sport or saving money, a realistic assessment of what is possible at any point, determination and consistency as well as allowing dreams to grow are all ingredients that need to be explored.

In your "dreams list" you will find out more about your uniqueness. It can be useful looking at other people's ideas but at the end of the day your dream list should reflect your desires. If it doesn't, you will not have the energy and motivation to turn the list into something that will add excitement, direction and colour to your life. I find when I look at other people's dream list then I am inspired and often want to include their ideas in my list. Some of them might stay on my list but there are others that I realise do not fit with who I am.

Another part of the process of working through and understanding your dreams is dealing with sabotage! If you do not place a value on yourself then the process is very difficult, you will end up with dreams that are easy to achieve and do not have any real cost attached, or no dreams at all. If there are no barriers you will probably have done them already so expect to find some challenges on the road. There is nothing sadder than unfulfilled promise. I remember one person who had been reminded of a childhood dream of being able to learn sign language and use it to support others. They investigated the opportunities available with excitement and energy but were never able to overcome their own internal barriers to take up the new adventure. They went back to the work that they were familiar with and never fulfilled their dream.

As we look at our dreams in the next chapter, remember that setting goals on the way to fulfilling dreams is important but they only become important after we have taken time to discover our dreams and not before.

To Do: Spend some time thinking back to when you were younger and dreamt like a child. To help with this, find some images that remind you of that stage of life, either old photos or pictures from the internet. Remember the excitement of the dreams that you had then. Start to dream again and even think of some seemingly impossible dreams. Go for a walk in a beautiful place and waste some time just day dreaming – make it a habit.

Chapter 3 – What are your Unclimbed Mountains? *(Nick Pengelly)*

"Go confidently in the direction of your dreams. Live the life you have imagined." Henry David Thoreau - writer and lifelong abolitionist, his books, articles, essays, journals, and poetry total over 20 volumes.

Brian has climbed more than one unclimbed mountain in recent years and had one occasion where the mountain had to remain unclimbed as the climb and the conditions conspired to make an ascent to the summit impossible. He still had a go. Each year there are more permits being made available for different mountains. We all need to give it a go.

In our lives, a dream list is not a final bucket list but it's our own personal workbook, like a diary written in outline ahead of time. It needs to be a working document, where we can add things, take them away, and record both our successes and partial successes. We will find that we will remember old dreams and realise that something that seemed important does not carry the weight it once had. The nice thing with the list is it belongs to you and you can use it in any way that suits you.

I have already referred to recording your dreams in the previous chapter. I have personally found it useful to have a dream book where I keep notes of the things that are important to me; it is something that I carry around with me. The downside with a note book is that I can easily lose it or put it on a shelf and forget about its existence. If it is going to work for you, then you need to find a way that is beneficial to you. For some people, keeping a list on your computer or phone is helpful, for others it works better including it in their diary; some people are more visual in the way they approach things so cutting out pictures or creating an online pin board is a great way of recording things. One of my children was showing me pictures of amazing places around the world recently; it was her dream list of places to visit. Above all, create a way that works for you. You might start by having a note book and then taking the key dreams and putting them on the fridge door. Use your imagination to find a method that inspires you and is useful for you as a reminder and you are able to apply daily.

In this chapter we are going to give you a simple framework to look at to enable you to identify your unclimbed mountains. The purpose of this framework is not to restrict you but to enable you to start thinking more about what dreams you may have. Some of you will have 100's of dreams written down and the challenge will be to hone them down to a more manageable list. For others, the challenge will be to avoid getting stuck behind the barriers of your current life to actually write anything down. It might be that you really struggle to dream at all and even thinking of one dream for your list is a struggle. Later in the book we address some of these blockages and how to work around them.

This is a process of finding the things that are really important to us, as they are the dreams we will be willing to change life to embrace, allocate time to and spend money on. Many people recommend finding 100 dreams with part of the reasoning that it will stretch your thinking and your imagination. I personally found that trying to get to a list of a hundred dreams became a bit like trying to pass a test. It was made worse when I watched my wife scribbling 100's of dreams down on her list. In the end I wanted to copy other people's lists just to have something to write down. (I still didn't put climbing an unclimbed mountain on my list though!) We have found that this number of 100 dreams becomes quite discouraging for many people and does not help them reach their end goal of doing something that adds enjoyment to or changes and shapes their lives. We are recommending that you find 21 different dreams. This will still stretch most people's thinking. It will challenge those of you who find it easy to write down 100's to refine your dreams to a level where you can actually get started.   The reality is most of us will not have the time to work on more than 2 or 3 dreams at any one time. Above all, remember that we are only creating a framework to start you thinking. With the target of 21 dreams we are suggesting 10 different categories with 2 dreams in each category so that you add richness to the whole of life and not limited areas. The final dream we are calling the Everest dream! This is the dream that may seem totally impossible. As you will see later, this might be very useful in drawing out some thoughts that are buried deep within you.

As you go through this process you may well find that there are some dreams that you can do something about so easily that you should just put down the pen and go and fulfil them. If you get a bit distracted researching a dream, that is allowed, just make sure you come back to the list before too long. Sometimes you just need to grab the moment. I had one of these dreams. I realised for 5 years I have talked about getting a pedigree silver tabby kitten. My excuse for not actually going ahead was our dog, appropriately named Mad dog. As she was a collie dog with that inbuilt need to round up anything that moved, we knew she would spend her life following the cat in a sheepdog manner. When we had previously had a cat, we used to watch the entertainment as the cat would outsmart the ever watching dog! Sadly, at the same time I began looking at my dreams, our dog suddenly died. The family immediately started thinking and looking for a new puppy and kitten. It was time to turn my dream into a reality. We quickly found a kitten that appeared quite promising and was available only 20 minutes down the road. We went off to look but despite the obvious attraction of this little thing and a very manipulative person trying to convince us to buy him, I knew it was not the dream. At this stage I could have bought any kitten, but that was not the point. A short time later we found kittens of the exact breed that I wanted. We now had to travel much further and it cost much more money but I could cross one thing off my dream list and make space for another dream. When the family's new puppy arrived the next weekend total chaos ensued between the kitten and the puppy; there are always aspects of dreams that you don't fully consider!

One my children kindly pointed out that I had been talking about having one of these pedigree kittens for at least 10 years, not the 5 years I had originally thought. It's a long time to wait to fulfil a simple dream that brings pleasure to the whole family. However, it was the simple process of committing my thoughts to paper that started the fulfilment of a dream and this is what we are looking at in this chapter.

Another dream on my list was to own a 50-year-old bonsai tree. I realised that I had already waited over 35 years to get a bonsai tree, all my adult life. As I am now over 50 years old, I knew I needed to purchase one that was at least 20 years old to enjoy the dream by the time I was 80 years old! When I investigated the price of trees that were 20 to 30 years old, the cost was certainly beyond my budget and the thought that despite my horticultural training I might accidently kill it made me decide not to buy one. A few weeks later I came into my office and there was this wonderful bonsai tree on my desk. Our friend Irene who heard me talking about bonsai trees left me a gift of a 38 year old tree that she had treasured for years and years and wanted to rehome. The challenge is on!

These are two smaller dreams that I have been able to fulfil very quickly. Some dreams are like this, they are easy to fulfil once we actually write them down as dreams we wish to pursue. During the running of a recent dreams course, each week people came back having completed some of their simpler dreams. These ranged from busking on the street, walking to certain places, winning games of chess to sorting out personal finance to enable them to have money to fulfil things of importance. The actual act of writing down or voicing our dreams allows us to start to fulfil them. Let's get started writing down and voicing out loud our unclimbed peaks so that we may climb them.

To help the process of identifying these 21 "unclimbed peaks", we have divided them down into the 10 dream categories with 2 dreams in each and then one final Everest dream. The second stage of the process is to then look at each dream and consider the time frame, finance involved and effort required to achieve it. Remember there is no right and wrong in this process so if you think something fits in a particular category then it does. You need to work on this in a way that suits your style and personality. It is unlikely that you will get very far unless you set aside some time to consider the process. Life can generally get so busy that we allow little time to think and to make changes. Fulfilling dreams is about moving away from our historical defaults in life to do something that is new and contains the adventure in life that we need. I find that I do this best when I have made a bit of space and am not rushing to do the next thing. This is where a workbook approach can be very useful.

We will briefly look at each category to give you an idea of things to look for. Even if you struggle to complete one category I would take the time needed to think and possibly deal with any blockages. For example, if you have always struggled financially, then it might feel a bit daunting to include something in the financial section. The reality is this could become a life changing section when some time, focus and mentoring might bring something from the impossible to the possible. We have seen when people have realised that owning their own home is possible by acknowledging their dream and finding out the financial possibilities rather than ignoring the desire in their hearts.

Our final category from the 10 categories is "Other". I am going to start here as this category more than any other highlights what we are hoping the book will help people achieve in life. We want to help people get out of the box of everyday life and live to the full and express that core DNA that makes them unique. This category is the one to make sure you are not boxed in; if your dream does not fit anywhere else put it here, at least for the time being. If you have a category that has more than 2 things in it and you just cannot separate a number of your priorities – list it here.

Key Categories:

<u>Other</u>

The place to put any dream you like!

<u>Relationships</u>

From a coffee with a friend to strengthening and renewing old acquaintances, this a rich and diverse category. It is so easy for life to drift or race by and we just don't have time to maintain our relationships. The importance of this category in people's lives is highlighted by the extensive use of social media but if this becomes a substitute for face to face time with people please stop and think a while. While this area might be one full of joy and opportunity to effectively engage the deep longings in our hearts it might also involve painful soul searching and there may be tears. If you are dreaming of restored relationships, it is well worth spending the time to understand and find healing for our own responses and reactions. We live in a society where many people have experienced breakdowns in their relationships with parents, siblings, relatives, partners and other important people in their lives. If in your heart you are looking for some restoration, those people should be on your list. Don't worry about the how at this stage but take note of your own inner responses as there may be something that you need to come back to. It might be on your dream list and the end of the day you cannot change things but at least you will have looked at them.

Other things to consider - making new friends, finding a life partner, re-discovering old friends that you have valued. Maybe you have an old-school friend that you have lost contact with and would love to contact again.

Maybe this is one of these areas you have given up on. It is in our human nature to avoid pain but if we avoid the pain sometimes associated with relationships or the lack of them then we also avoid the hope and fulfilment that could be ours. I have sat with many people as their lives draw to a close and conversation is always around family and friends, regrets and things that they wish they had put right. I have also seen people at funerals pondering the loss of someone they have not seen for years and wish they had contacted.

I have included my family in my list of dreams. Over the past couple of years my children have started to form their own lives and discover their own dreams. Increasingly I have realised that my children could live anywhere in the country and my daughter and her husband may well choose to live in another country. My wife and I are planning life in a way that we will be able to engage fully with our children, and maybe one day, our grandchildren, wherever they are in the world.

We cannot expect our children to always come in our direction, we may need to go to where they are.

There is a wonderful parable in the bible that refers to a treasure buried in a field. The person goes off and buys the field so that he can get the treasure. In the category of relationships, how much field are you willing to buy to get hold of your treasure. Take your time on this one, and be honest with yourself.

Places

Over the years I have realised that I enjoy going places, am often challenged by them and I always love being home again. By the time I was 18 years old I had made one trip overseas; it was a school trip to France. Since then I have had the privilege of going to many interesting and out of the way places. I have realised it is not just going somewhere that I enjoy but being able to connect with local people and experience something of their culture and life. This is something that through church linked missions I have been able to do. Sitting with pastors on a very remote island near Bougainville, Papua New Guinea, eating local food talking with someone who had taken 36 hours on a boat to get from his remote island in the middle of the ocean to our meeting is pretty amazing. Even if my list was short of ideas, I know that this is one category where my wife is likely to have enough places on her list to fill any gaps on mine.

Do you have places that you would love to visit either locally or further afield? I was talking with one of my daughters who showed me her growing collection of photos from different countries around the world. When I asked her why she had collected them, she told me that they were all places that she wanted to visit. On my list is to take my wife on a trip around Cornwall to the places I visited as a child. My wife who loves travelling, has dozens of places that she would like to go around the world which include seeing the Northern lights, visiting Iceland and driving Route 66 in America. As you can see from Brian's list later, he would like to go to slightly more extreme places and has completed all of the above and more. If you are someone who has lots of places that you would like to visit, then select at least one that is achievable in a shorter time frame and one that will take significant planning. At some point my wife and I would like to travel across Australia in a campervan. That's not going to happen tomorrow but can feature in our dreams.

Natalie dreamt for many years of going to Egypt. This for her was her Everest dream. When the opportunity actually did come to go and spend some time working with children in extreme poverty in Egypt, she still had to grab the opportunity, raise the money and go. She describes it as a beautiful experience that she could never have imagined happening; touching a pyramid, seeing Tutankhamen's gold, working with children, all fulfilling her dream.

Finances

"I can't afford to" is a phrase used over and over. How many times has finance been a limitation in our lives? If you are thinking I can't have financial dreams as I am in debt and have no spare money, you may already have found your starting point. Getting out of debt can be very difficult as in most cases it is going to demand some very significant life changes. There are some great organisations such as Christians Against Poverty (CAP) that can help you sort your finances, help you produce budgets and finally clear your debt. As part of the dreaming process this is so worth doing. Imagine if the money that is being used to pay interest on a debt could be put towards your dreams instead. One person who was in debt describes the impact of this on her life. It left her feeling depressed as she could not see a way out. It meant that she could not give gifts to her friends and at times avoided going out with friends because of the cost. At this point, there seemed no reason to dream as everything needed money. She went to CAP who gave a tiny window of hope and then helped with budgets and liaised with creditors. This lady related the joy of finally, after several years, becoming debt free. Lots of other things that had been put on hold could now be considered again and she could start the simple pleasure of giving small gifts to her friends on their birthdays.

The founder of Christians against Poverty (CAP), John Kirkby, has written about his own inspirational story in the book "Nevertheless" subtitled "The incredible story of one man's mission to change thousands of people's lives." John writes openly about his own struggle with debt and the emotional cost it took on him.

"In early 1992 my whole world fell apart. I made many mistakes and had borrowed huge sums of money from banks to finance my business operations. Banks started to ask for their money back and the house I had built plummeted in value before I could sell it. I might have

looked fine on the outside but inside I was a broken, lonely man watching all he had worked for being lost before his very eyes."

It was out of this time and the process John went through to sort out his own financial situation that the dream was born to help others out of their financial difficulties. The full and challenging story is well documented in his book. This is a dream that continues to grow and expand with around 300 centres offering debt advice and over 100 job clubs and other initiatives. A recent press release from CAP clearly shows the benefit of their rounded approach as 93% of people interviewed had managed to stay out of debt.

Don't let circumstances become the barbed wire fence around your dreams. Your dreams are not only about yourself but can have a massive impact for good on your family, friends, and in the world around you.

The newspapers and current affairs programmes are full of the need to save money for your retirement. When you are 15 years old it seems too far off to think about and you may only have money from a weekend job; when you are 50 years old you may wish that you had started saving sooner. This is only one aspect of financial planning. In fact it would be a good idea for financial advisers to go through a dream list with people before helping them put together a financial plan. Many of our dreams will require finance and this might involve some conflict of priorities; the process of thinking them through will help bring some helpful clarity. This is also an area that changes quite considerably at different stages of life.

It might be that you need to set a plan to save a small amount of money each month towards one of your life goals but we will cover this in Chapter 6 with "Taking steps to the summit". For now, do not worry about financial barriers but just dream and commit these dreams to paper.

It takes financial planning to buy your own home, or to have the pension to retire at 55 as Brian would like to do (see Brian's Dream's 21 list below).

I have been thinking through my financial goals with my wife. When my daughter got married, my wife and I realised we would need to do some planning if we were going to be actively involved in their lives as they looked to fulfil one of their dreams of living and working overseas. A few years ago I set up a business with a friend with one of its long term aims to earn some extra income to assist with this. There are many ways that you can make a little extra income if you need it to fulfil life dreams.

Under finance, you may also want to consider the whole subject of legacy. This comes in a number of different ways. If you have children, grandchildren or other family members and friends you may want to think though what sort of financial legacy you would like to provide for them during your lifetime and even through your estate. There is also a legacy that is left through the support of charities. One of the thoughts I often have and this may well end up on my dream list is how the charities that I support will continue to be supported after I have died. The area of legacy can be included in many other categories. I would encourage each one of us to think about how we can do something to help others, not just in a financial manner but also through giving our time and skills. We may not be able to do what Brian dreams of by helping others raise £1 million for charity (see Brian's Dream's 21 list below) but think about something that is important to you and maybe include that in your dream list.

Work

I love my work; I lead a local church and have the opportunity to share in people's lives through exciting and successful times as well as in the incredibly difficult and challenging times that can come along. It is through my work that I have realised how much I enjoy helping people climb their unclimbed mountains by finding, expressing and fulfilling their dreams. This particularly applies to the workplace. I have always had a passion for business and wanted the opportunity to run my own business. On my own this was unlikely to happen as the church work left little space for anything else. It was one day when I was driving along that the name of the business came to mind "JustSeed". That evening I purchased the domain name plus a few similar names and the business to sell seeds was conceived but not yet started. It was while talking to one of my friends Arnold about the idea that he said that his wife Sue would love to be involved in a business like that. The partnership was born, an ideal combination, as Sue has many skills that would be needed for success and Arnold had the vital skill of speaking his mind. Arnold was our strongest critic but biggest supporter. The business developed slowly with my input either early in the morning or in front of the television late in the evening. My wife, also called Sue, reluctantly watched the kitchen table being taken over for a while before we moved the business to its own premises and the employment of quality staff brought my sanity back. The journey from initial dream through reality to stability took a number of years. It did not happen by magic but hard work combined with an undoubted blessing of God has seen the business grow and grow. Above all, it has and continues to be a great place of helping people find their dreams and their future.

If you have a dream of a business and you invest everything, you must be sure of success or at the end you have nothing. If you can test the waters of your dream as we were able to with limited investment and no debt, your small business could provide the dream fund. We started by investing under £200 and the time we and our long suffering families had to give.

Amanda has held a dream for over 25 years to be an art therapist. It has been a dream where every step has been full of battles. Initially the battle to get started was tough as she had to enrol on an MA course without a degree. The whole journey was also challenged when Amanda fell seriously ill with a rare illness. In spite of these battles, Amanda started to make a rare recovery from her illness, enrolled onto the course and even got the necessary work placement. The dream is not yet complete as Amanda still needs to finish her qualification. She describes it as,

"quite a journey, sometimes it feels as though I have passed through the eye of a hurricane".

When you look at your future, your work place, what are your ambitions; are you looking for promotion, training, different opportunities, career change, to start a business, or to build your existing business? We spend too much of our lives in our workplaces to allow it to be stagnant and uninspiring for too long.

Possessions

And why not? There is something in me that likes to collect things. One of my dreams on my dream's 21 list was to own a painting by Sir Peter Scott, the world famous ornithologist. I was brought up near the Slimbridge Wildfowl Trust in Gloucestershire and visited regularly when I was young, admiring many of his paintings that hang there. When I developed my initial dream list, this dream was on my list. A quick look at the prices of the originals made me realise that I would have to shelve that idea at this stage but I have instead now purchased my first signed print of a Sir Peter Scott painting at auction. That's where my interest in collecting started and I have plenty of space for a few more prints. I have a friend who seems to buy every lonely garden fork or spade that needs a bit of restoration. He has enough in his shed to support an army of workers. We are all completely different so take some time to decide what should be on your dream list. Is there something that you would like to own or even collect?

Activities

This is one point where Brian and I overlap as this book is the result of a dream that we both had. Our approaches are very different but together we will get to our goal and produce something that we hope will inspire and help many people. This category is very broad but can include anything that you

want to do in life. It's a great category to add something that is
more challenging or requires a bit more training and effort to
achieve. They are things that you plan for your enjoyment and
possibly challenge as well. You may also wish to consider some
areas where you can impact others through supporting
charitable work through your efforts and how you can impact
the lives of other people.

Achievements

To achieve something, it has to have a connection and
motivation from deep inside. It cannot be something that is
just a good idea or even someone else's idea. This might seem
obvious but often we do not complete something because we
have not found an internal energy and drive. My Mum was a
very good pianist and played for her own enjoyment. She felt
that music was important and made it a priority to get each
one of her children to play a musical instrument. In the case of
my older brother the initial encouragement and input has
given him a skill which he continues to use today. In my case
there was no connection and the idea of practicing each day
was something to be avoided at all cost. It was not unusual for
me to arrive at my piano lesson for the teacher to tell me that
he had had my mum on the phone again to apologise for my
lack of practice. The only reason that I kept going as long as I
did was I enjoyed the company of the piano teacher who was
also a fanatical cricket fan. My attempts at learning the viola
also failed to impress. My teacher regularly shouted at me and
complained at my lack of musical ability and that I would
always regret not putting the effort in. I would not put learning
a musical instrument on my list as I did not make the necessary

connection, but it might be one of your lifetime aims. Take time to think of the things that would inspire you, it might be a language or a personal best at sport. The list is endless.

Experiences

This is a great category and is designed to add some fun and entertainment to your life. In my list I have tried to find a couple of things that I will need to make an effort to accomplish. I could also have added many other things to my list including watching certain sports live and visiting places. One of the experiences that will not be on my list will be going on a rollercoaster. I have included one thing that with a small amount of planning is possible and another experience which will require quite a bit of planning and also saving money. Brian has put climbing another Unclimbed Mountain on his list and by the time we have completed the book he will hope to have achieved this. However, I think it will still stay on his list as he searches for another Unclimbed Mountain and focuses on the next adventure. Add the experiences you really want to have in this category.

Personality

Is there something about yourself that you would like to develop or change? This category includes the whole area of personal development which can be physical, emotional and spiritual. As a Christian I am very aware of the personal need to grow and develop in an ongoing fashion. To do this well there is a need to deal with past issues that hold us back as well as have an awareness of things we want to grow in moving forward. Many people I meet are held back in areas of their lives because of previous life experiences. There are currently several television programmes helping people deal with weight problems and this is very on trend. Many times, however, personal issues such as weight, body appearance, and character are associated with things that have happened in our past life. The people that get the real long term breakthroughs are often those who face the history and find some type of peace so they can live differently today. We deal with the impact of blockages later in the book. If you are aware of personal blockages in life, life draining things, why not have the courage to include one of them on your list and later decide the best way of resolving the issues. Some of the personality things you might like to think about in this category might include some area of spiritual development, if you are a Christian reading the bible, developing a prayer life or finding a local church community might be relevant. Other ideas include creating regular space for personal thought or meditation and rest, writing a life diary, developing an inner peace, dealing with an anger issue. The list is endless and very personal. These examples above are all linked to an inner development but you might have a physical development dream in your life. Many people dream of weighing the same as when they were young; I am one of them and this is something that is a bit of a challenge as I love tasting new foods, particularly when they are from different cultures. I have set myself a long term dream of significantly reducing my weight and increasing my fitness. One of my fitness aims was to walk 12,000 steps a day. My daily work has an office, coffee facilities, colleague's offices and a bathroom only 20 steps in each direction. My lifestyle can easily become sedentary. Initially it was easy to get to 12,000 steps as I would walk every day with my son but when he moved away from home and the nights became darker, it became far more challenging. My motivation is simple, I want to live as long and healthy a life as possible! This 12,000 steps is quite specific but my dream is to get fitter and I only use it as an illustration. Do not worry at this point about any specifics regarding your dreams as we will deal with this later in how to break your dream down into specific goals.

When you have spent some time developing your list there are few things that we would recommend you do to improve and develop your list.

If you are someone who finds it easy to dream then the challenge will be to reduce your list to those that are truly connected to your heart, those that really excite you and provide you with a drive to complete them. You might not want to remove any if you have more than 21, so just put them on a secondary list as you will need them when you have started to fulfil your top 21.

If you are struggling to complete you list then hopefully the following process will provoke some more ideas and help you to discover the dreams that are really important to you.

We would recommend you find someone who knows you well and take some time and share the dreams on your list with them. This is an important step because the process of talking will highlight the dreams that are truly important to you. There are some subjects that I am enthusiastic about and will talk enthusiastically about for hours – if I can find someone to listen. One of our boys has a hobby of collecting football cards, he has hundreds of them and is always ready to buy more. If you ask about any of the players at the top level, he can tell you their names, which club, where they came from, which position they play; his energy is incredible. If he was making his list, then I think football would be in most categories! You may also find that the process of talking about your dreams will open up a range of new ideas and stimulate dreams that had been forgotten.

As part of this process I would encourage you to take one of your dreams and enlarge it. Take it from the realms of possibility to the realms of impossibility. This process is about opening yourself up to discover the depths of your dreams. Most of us tend to hold back, either to avoid the possibility of failure, because we think it's impossible anyway or simply because we don't want others to think we have got too big for our boots. Dream big, then dream a bit bigger.

By the way, you don't have to wait until you have read the book to start fulfilling your dreams, we have found that many people can accomplish some of their dreams straight away. Even the process of recording the dream somehow makes it possible. This is where it is great doing this as a group as people can encourage each other to start taking some action. Within the first few weeks of running a "Dreams Workshop", we found many people coming back the next session already having completed some of their life dreams. This included a number of people booking holidays, walking in the autumn leaves, busking in a local city for fun, walking along the conjunction of 2 rivers, contacting old friends, buying a pet, cooking, writing, decluttering the house, asking for help to deal with personal history, buying a Christmas tree, and losing weight. The list goes on. The energy and satisfaction among the group grew in just a few weeks.

If you have completed a dream, make sure you record it and how it made you feel. This personal journal will help to inspire you when progress is a little slower. It also gives you space to add something new in your working list of 21 Dreams.

When you have developed your list of 21 dreams there is one more step we would like you to take.

We would like you to put each of your dreams in one of four categories. The categories reflect the level of challenge that each dream represents to you. You should end up with some dreams in each category.

Moderate

This is the first category. Initially, we were going to call this the easy category but realised that there is probably a reason why we have not already completed the dreams on our list so they are not "easy". The blockage may be simple to deal with but it will take some effort. In this category you should include any dreams that you can accomplish with a little bit of time, effort and maybe some planning. It should be something that you can do without the need for significant financial planning. Brian has included in this list, contacting University friends, something that may take a bit of work to get contact details. I recently did this with an old friend in America, through the power of social media and it was not long before I was back in touch with someone who I'd wanted to contact.

Challenging

This category will contain your dreams that may take longer to fulfil. This might be because there is the need for more planning and effort and/or it may require some financial planning and saving to make it possible. If you are in debt but have the income to sort the problem out, then this might be a good category to place a debt free dream in. It is certainly going to require some time to prepare a budget and it is going to take effort to stick to the budget. It might take a couple of years to clear outstanding debt. If the situation is particularly difficult it may be worth getting expert help to sort things out.

Tough

This is the place for the longer-term dreams, those that are much more complicated to complete involving more time and a sustained effort. Often one of the limitations is financial so it might take some longer term financial planning to make them happen. You may dream of a certain job or career path that involves a study course or attending university with all the associated costs. Maybe you would love to take a long holiday travelling to the other side of the world. This could stay as a pipe dream that never happens or you could start the planning now knowing it will be many years before you can accomplish the dream. It might take years to save the money, gain special permission from your work place to take an extended time off work, then there is the detailed planning of where you are going to go and what you are going to do when you get there. Another example might be planning to purchase your own house. Again planning is vital but I have seen a number of times where a dream that seemed tough or impossible becomes possible because by having the courage to start planning, people have found their dream is closer than they thought. What seemed tough then became challenging.

Extreme

This is your "Everest Dream". At this point is seems impossible for a whole variety of reason, it might be financially beyond your capabilities, your current stage of life does not allow it to happen, or you might not currently have the skills or experience to get beyond base camp. Everything about it is beyond your wildest dreams. Even writing it down might be a challenge. Imagine how you would feel if you complete this one. The tears, the laughter, the stories you would have to tell. Later on we will examine how we start to unpack these deep dreams to see if we can help you get beyond base camp into your realms of the impossible.

Again, let me emphasise that this is a personal activity with no right and wrong way of completing it. Each of us will have different perceptions of what is moderate, challenging, or tough. For one person the idea of learning a new language might be a joy and pleasure, for the next person it is a dream they have but will be a tough one to fulfil. My daughter enjoys learning new languages, I certainly don't.

If you have completed this breakdown of categories and find that all your dreams fall in the Moderate or at the other extreme, the Tough category, then we would suggest that you review your list of 21 dreams.

If everything is in the moderate category, then there is room to dream a bit bigger and bolder. It might take a bit of time but look at your dreams and see if you can push them further out of your comfort zone. It might be that your day to day financial situation is very tight so you have avoided anything that requires much money; why not look again and include some tough dreams that require financial input.

At the other end of the scale, if all your dreams are in the Tough category, then you will need to find some more Moderate dreams that you can fulfil in a short time span. This will build you a history of fulfilling dreams and some stories that will encourage you in your pursuit of more challenging options.

Here is someone's story to encourage your journey:

Emma had a dream from the age of 16 years old which she believed would be impossible to achieve. She longed to go to Africa and experience the culture and work with children and young people. This was an extreme dream for Emma. It was 10 years before an opportunity came to be part of a team to go to Kenya. Even at this point there were many obstacles to be overcome. There were the internal challenges of overcoming fear and even believing the dream could be realised with regards finance. The team working together were able to fund raise and make the journey possible. The right team leader created a feeling of security. The trip turned into an adventure of a lifetime, including an upgrade to business class on the outward journey and amazing opportunities to volunteer with a local charity. It left Emma dreaming of one day going back.

To Do: Find a place where you won't be disturbed and take some time for yourself. Take the time to write out your

"Dreams 21". To start with don't try and categorise them, just get writing, if you have more ideas keep writing. When you have completed this, try and use the 10 categories to put 2 dreams into each + 1 x "Everest" dream in any category. The categories are listed below:

Relationships; Possessions; Places; Activities; Experiences; Personality; Work; Finances; Achievements; Other.

Now break these down into the following categories: Moderate (will take little time and effort, may need some planning); Challenging (may take a longer time, involve more planning and effort, may involve finance); Tough (longer term, will involve a lot of planning, finance, time and effort); Extreme (Your 1 x Everest Dream). We will all have different perceptions of what is moderate, challenging, or tough, therefore make your dream list personal to you. Some people find it better to work and talk with other people as they go through making a list to get more inspiration. There is no hard and fast way to do this, find your own way.

To help you with this, please see the lists below from both Brian's and Nick's Dreams 21 list.

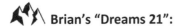 **Brian's "Dreams 21":**

Relationships
- Get in touch with old University friends
- Get on better with both my mum and mother-in-law

Possessions

- Log cabin retreat in the UK
- Old classic Harley Davidson

Places

- Visit Antarctica
- Visit Alaska

Activities

- Complete a sprint triathlon
- Write a book on achieving dreams

Experiences

- Climb another Unclimbed Mountain
- See a tiger in the wild

Personality/Image

- Lose 1.5 stone (10 kilos/22lbs)
- Get a 6 pack

Work

- Raise £1million for charity in a year
- Get 10 overseas and 10 UK challenges on the books in a year

Finances

- Retire by 55
- Make enough money to be able to support more charitable giving

Achievements

- Learn Spanish
- Lead a large group of people to the summit of an unclimbed mountain
- Dog sled to the North Pole (Everest Dream)

Other

- Move to Spain to retire
- Leave behind a legacy of people who have fulfilled their dreams and reached their potential

Dream Categories:

Moderate
- Get in touch with old University friends
- Complete a sprint triathlon

Challenging
- Get on better with both my mum and mother-in-law
- Lose 1.5 stone (10kilos/22lbs)
- Get a 6 pack
- Learn Spanish
- Get 10 overseas and 10 UK challenges on the books in a year
- Write a book on achieving dreams
- Visit Alaska
- Old classic Harley Davidson
- Raise £1million for charity in a year

Tough
- Move to Spain to retire
- Retire by 55
- Make enough money to be able to support more charitable giving
- Lead a large group of people to the summit of an unclimbed mountain
- See a tiger in the wild
- Climb another Unclimbed Mountain
- Visit and camp on Antarctica
- Log cabin retreat in the UK
- Leave behind a legacy of people who have fulfilled their dreams and reached their potential

Extreme (Everest Dream)
- Dog sled to North Pole

Nick's "Dreams 21":

Relationships

- Visit American friends old and new
- Prioritise my family, wherever they are in the world

Possessions

- A piece of land for an orchard, vegetables and animals.
- Own an original Sir Peter Scott painting
- Own a 50 year old Bonsai tree

Places

- Take my wife around Cornwall
- Revisit Long Island New York

Activities

- Grow a giant pumpkin (500lb plus to start)
- Publish a novel (Everest Dream)

Experiences

- Eat in Tom Kerridge's Michelin starred restaurant
- Experience wildlife on the Galapagos Islands

Personality

- Maintain weight within my BMI
- Walk an average 12,000 steps a day

Work

- Have an impact in the local community
- Double business turnover and be the largest online Seed retailer.

Finances

- Plan retirement income

-   Have a fund to continue supporting the favourite charities long after my death

Achievements

-   Name all wild animals and plants in local area
-   Become a holder of National Collection of Plant Species

Other

-   Breed a new plant variety
-   Own an Alpine House

Dream Categories:

Moderate

-   Planning retirement income
-   Eat in Tom Kerridge's Michelin starred restaurant
-   A piece of land for an orchard, vegetables and animals.
-   Take my wife around Cornwall
-   Revisit Long Island New York
-   Prioritise my family, wherever they are in the world

Challenging

-   Visit American friends old and new
-   Become a holder of National Collection of Plant species
-   Name all wild animals and plants in local area
-   Own an Alpine House
-   Have an impact in the local community
-   Double business turnover and be the largest online Seed retailer.
-   Maintain weight within my BMI

Tough

- Walk an average of 12,000 steps a day
- Grow a giant pumpkin (500lb plus to start)
- Own a 50 year old bonsai tree

- Have a fund to continue supporting favourite charities long after my death
- Own an original Sir Peter Scott painting
- Breed a new Plant Variety
- Experience wildlife on Galapagos Islands

Extreme (Everest Dream)
- Publish a novel

Chapter 4 – Sharing the Climb *(Brian Jackson)*

"Few things in the world are more powerful than a positive push, a smile, a word of optimism and hope, a "you can do it" when things are tough." Richard M de Vos – Co-founder of Amway, owner of Orlando Magic NBA team and US Billionaire.

"The greatest good you can do for another is not just to share your riches but to reveal to him his own." Benjamin Disraeli – British Politician and writer, who twice served as UK Prime Minister.

Just as it is extremely hard to climb an unclimbed mountain with no assistance, achieving dreams is often far easier with other people joining you on your journey, sharing the climb. Chhubohe, my first unclimbed mountain, was climbed with a group of 3 from the UK, 2 climbing Sherpas, a cook crew, camp Sherpas and muleteers; in total a team of 11 people to put just 4 on the summit. Your dreams may be very personal but having someone sharing the climb with you is one of the keys to achieving a successful summit of completing your dream.

One of the unclimbed mountains in both Nick and my dreams list was losing weight. Let us use that as an example to demonstrate how we need other people to share the climb with us.

My story: I decided as part of my mid-life concerns at 48 that I would go to the GP and have a standard check up on my body a body MOT. This was not of course all my own doing as my wife had actually "suggested" I do this. I followed up on this "suggestion" and ended up getting everything checked from my cholesterol to my body fat, my BMI to my visceral fat (fat around my major organs) and my maturation age (the age my body is equal to with regards all the previous readings). I was not excited to hear that my 48 year old body had a maturation age of 56! Until this check-up, I had thought many times about losing weight but had not really had the motivation as I wanted to lose weight but I was also happy and content with my lifestyle. I always dreamt that I would lose weight but never actually turned this into a plan or did anything about that dream. I now had the motivation to see this dream fulfilled but I would need some assistance to complete it. I needed some people to share the journey, to share the climb with me. I decided on a 3 month plan to lose 10 kilos (1.5 stone or 22 lbs). I got in touch with a friend who is involved with weight loss programmes and asked for him to assist me. He was my first fellow climber on this unclimbed mountain of mine. To do this in 3 months, I was going to need to substitute 2 x meals per day (breakfast and lunch) with protein shakes instead of my normal diet and then have a high protein meal in the evenings. This would involve buying lots of chicken as well as quorn, quinoa and other protein rich food. As my wife, Steph, is a vegetarian and we normally eat veggie food at home, I now needed to speak to Steph to see if she was happy to support me in this and change our weekly shop; she then became my second support climber. These fellow climbers grew and grew as other friends found out what I was doing. They encouraged me in not drinking a glass of wine with them (actually they just didn't pour me one when they had theirs), when eating out of an evening at friends' houses they would not give me a dessert or just not make one so I wasn't missing out. This assistance all added up to me having many others sharing the climb with me, offering me accountability to them as well as to myself for what I was doing and this eased the climb and made the dream that much easier to fulfil. I can happily say that 3 months down the line, I have lost ...., well let's leave that for now as I would like to come back to that later.

Nick's story:

"When you like good food and you like eating out, trying to lose weight is always going to be a challenge. When you have been brought up to always clear your plate then the challenge is even harder. I have often tried to lose weight but as for many people my difficulty is keeping the weight off having lost it. This is an issue on many people's minds and this is illustrated by how many people go to clubs and how many different types of diets there are. It is worth pointing out that the clubs must work to some extent as people would not continue attending. They help you formulate your dream and provide you with a weekly opportunity to check your progress and receive some more encouragement and tips. I have never tried a club but knew I needed to do something before I gave up on checking the scales. I set myself a couple of very simple goals. The diet always restarted on a Monday morning. I always find it easier to diet effectively during the week and then try to maintain the loss at the weekend. My second goal was to weigh less at the end of the year than I did at the beginning of the year until I got inside my

optimum BMI level. My real goal was not so much weight loss but maximising the length and health of my time on this earth!

__It's been a journey of success and then times when things have not gone so well.__ I have deliberately given myself breaks at times when I have known that trying to keep to a diet would just be demoralising. After 3 years I am not quite inside my optimum BMI but consistently far closer than I was.

I know if someone had told me I needed to lose weight they would have seen my stubborn side but when I had decided I wanted to lose weight I was only going to achieve the goal with the support of other people. It was not something that I would ever do in isolation. The first thing I had to do was tell my wife, Sue, as this would significantly alter the food we ate. I still grumbled a bit when I was told I did not need dessert! It also meant we had to change some of our time together as we both like a drink and a piece of cake. I then made my personal challenge part of the conversation in the office and at home. It's much harder to cheat when you have other people looking out for you."

As can be seen from both these stories, even a seemingly straightforward and simple dream affects others around us and we need to ask these people to share the climb with us in order for us to be able to achieve our dreams. Informing others of our dreams also has the very positive side effect of giving us accountability to that person. We have shared a dream with another person and now they become motivated to check up on our progress, to encourage, cajole, sometimes to reprimand but always standing there alongside us, sharing the climb. Sharing your dream with someone is the best way to start achieving those dreams. The action of sharing your dream will kick start the dream by making you accountable to someone else.

"I am a success today because I had a friend who believed in me and I didn't have the heart to let him down". Abraham Lincoln - 16th US President.

Another side effect of sharing your dream with others is that once you have shared your dream with a friend or family member, the dream is out in the open, it is no longer a secret wish but a fully-fledged declared dream; it is now not only in your heart but in the open arena. This can of course make us vulnerable as dreams are heart issues and deeply personal but it is also very powerful to share our dreams, allow ourselves to become vulnerable and gain fellow climbers to share the climb. As there is a vulnerability and openness required in sharing your dreams, how and who you choose as your fellow climbers is one of the keys to your success in achieving the dream. Think very carefully about who you want along on the journey with you, who can be of true help and assistance. There are several categories of person you can choose from and I have described just four of these below:

- Someone with the same or similar dream
- A close friend or family member who you know still has their own dreams and can therefore be supportive of your dreams

- A mentor - a more mature dreamer, a more experienced climber to support you and mentor you through the process of dreaming
- Passing strangers

Each of these can support you in different ways. Let me illustrate how each different category of fellow climber can be of assistance to you and therefore help you in completing your dream.

Someone with the same or similar dream

The person with the same or similar dream is able to set similar goals as you do and you can then compare and support each other along the way as you may well experience similar obstacles that you need to overcome. You will be able to share and celebrate successes along the climb and share ways in which you may have overcome an obstacle with your fellow climber and they can do the same for you. This will become a mutual journey with healthy competition and co-operation.

A close friend or family member who you know still has their own dreams and can therefore be supportive of your dreams

A close friend or work colleague is going to know you well and therefore may well be an easier person with whom to share your dreams, with less risk of vulnerability. They will be supportive and could become a prayer partner in your climb. You may need your close friends or work colleagues to know the dream so that they can support any changes in your life with regards finance or time. If you need to save more money, build up annual leave or take more time out of your normal day to fulfil your dream, this may necessarily mean less time to spend with your friends and work colleagues and they can only be supportive of this if they are on board with your dream.

N.B. Be cautious of close friends who would hem you in, who will not support you. It can happen that your closest friends do not want you to be fulfilling dreams and then possibly and probably changing as a person. They may enjoy the status quo of their relationship with you as it is and not want any change to occur. They may also not want their own behaviour challenged by you fulfilling dreams when they are not. You will know of the friends or work colleagues who when you are trying to get fitter or trying to lose weight, still try and pressure you into having the extra pint at the pub or the big dessert on the menu at a meal. They want to hem you in because they wish you to stay the same and it allows them to be happy and content with the status quo and not be personally challenged. They may also stop or hinder you through the false belief that they are protecting you, that they have your best interests at heart. They may not want to see you fail and be disheartened or get hurt and therefore are not supportive of your dreams.

A family member, especially someone within the same household such as a parent or partner, may well be necessary to have as your fellow climber as you may need him or her to change and adapt along with you to allow you to fulfil your dream as demonstrated in the losing weight examples.

A mentor - a more mature dreamer, a more experienced climber to support you and mentor you through the process of dreaming

A mentor, someone who is a seasoned dream achiever, can provide help in so many areas of your climb. They have achieved dreams in the past and can be inspirational in their support as well as extremely practical. A mentor can provide support with detailed planning and the breakdown of each step to take to achieve the dream, highlighting and helping overcome obstacles, both those that are self-imposed and those that arise externally, offering motivational support when necessary and affording the necessary accountability. Choosing a mentor can be a difficult process so I will defer to an expert who I have had the privilege of getting to know on three charity cycle challenges, Leon Taylor, Olympic Silver Medallist, Motivational Speaker, and mentor to Tom Daley, Olympic Diver, amongst others. Leon has written an excellent book about Mentoring called "Mentor", a really insightful read. I will, with his permission, paraphrase some key areas of mentoring that I wish to highlight from his book to enable you to choose a good mentor. If you wish to know more about mentoring, then I would advise you to purchase his book.

Firstly, there is not a one-size-fits-all approach to mentoring and a good mentor should be flexible enough to be able to choose different methods of mentoring that support you.

Secondly, a mentor should offer support to you along your journey but not only support; they should also be able to gently challenge you to promote determination, drive, focus, motivation, and possibly even temporary frustration.

Thirdly, a mentor should be able to encourage you into clarity of purpose and action by provoking how you make decisions, to become more decisive, as to not make a decision to do something is to decide to do nothing.

Lastly, I would like to quote Leon directly on how mentors should be story tellers who promote you to think about how you set your goals, how you achieve your dreams.

"When I was younger, I had to make a choice between two mentors that I had worked with in the past. They were very different. One was really helpful; I would tell him/her what was bothering me at the time and he/she would provide a really helpful suggestion – an immediate fix. It was very efficient. I asked a question, got an answer, didn't need to think much, just did what he/she said, and that was it. I struggle to find an example now. I can't really remember anything he/she told me, but it was great at the time. The other one was much more frustrating. I just wanted to find an answer to my question, a quick fix, but he/she would never give me straightforward advice – it was really frustrating. He/she would ask me questions that really made me think and sometimes I didn't get it until the next day, or sometimes even longer. He/she would tell stories that were really interesting but seemed a bit off-topic. But the funny thing is that I remember them – I remember so many of his/her little phrases and life lessons and when I look back now, they made a massive difference. If you were in my shoes, which would you have chosen?" Leon Taylor – Olympic Silver Medallist Diver and author of the book "Mentor".

Passing strangers

Even passing strangers can have an influence on your dreams, can inspire you or can prompt you to dream and they are part of your team sharing your climb with you, even if for just the briefest moment. To illustrate this, let me tell you an incredible story of 'coincidence' and dreaming. Over to Dave Cooke, who used to work as the International Projects Manager for Samaritan's Purse, is the founder of the charity, Teams 4 U, and co-founder of Operation Christmas Child.

"A few years ago I was working in the Crimea on a team refurbishing wards for the children's hospital of infectious diseases in Simferopol. I needed to get to the hospital so I flagged down a taxi and a battered old Lada turned up and I jumped in the back. The young man driving turned around and stared at me. He then asked, 'Are you Dave Cooke?' and when I said yes he replied 'You probably don't remember me, I'm Sergei.' He then went on to tell me that I'd met him years ago in the sewers whilst he was living on the streets. We'd run a programme meeting these abandoned children who slept on the pipes under the city to keep warm and we had given them gifts in shoeboxes and played football with them. Sergei reminded me that I'd taken him to McDonalds and he said to me 'You made me feel 6ft tall. Before, I could only run around McDonalds like the stray dogs and take food from the bins. Do you remember what you said to me?' I, of course, replied 'No, Sergei, it was a long time ago, I cannot remember'. He told me that I'd asked him what his dream was! I've asked so many children that question! Sergei reminded me he'd

answered that he wanted to be a taxi driver but that as a child living on the streets, this seemed nigh on impossible. However, here he was so many years later fulfilling his dream.

*It's always made me wonder how many more children and other people passing by we may have inspired to believe that they can achieve their dreams by just asking them the simple question, **What is your dream?***"

Using one, many or all the categories above, hopefully you will now be able to look for fellow climbers to share the climb with you and cajole, encourage and support you in fulfilling your dreams. One area that you may not think would be a good place to recruit fellow climbers would be from those who have stopped dreaming. You would normally want to avoid any person who has stopped dreaming, as they could be a hindrance rather than a supporter on your climb. People who have given up on dreaming can be extremely negative about others having dreams as they may well have been hurt by not fulfilling their own dreams. They would therefore not usually be a good choice of fellow climber on your ascent.

"Keep away from people who try to belittle your ambition. Small people always do that. But the really great make you feel that you, too, can become great." Mark Twain – Adventurer and author.

However, occasionally, the actual act of inviting such a person to share your climb could also inspire them to dream themselves so choose very carefully and wisely who you want to share the climb with you. You may well be surprised with who you eventually choose.

To Do: To help you fulfil your dreams by gaining fellow climbers, choose a moderate, challenging, and tough dream from your dream list. Using each of these 3 dreams, write down a list besides each of them as to who could possibly share the climb with you. It would be great to have a fellow climber on the journey who also shares the same dream as you and then you can assist each other in the climb. Consider whom you would like to stand alongside you in support, prayer, or regular meetings. When you have completed this list, write a second list of who you may need to have on the climb with you to enable it to be successful, to actually achieve the dream? The dream may involve finance, if so, your parents, partner, spouse or even bank manager may need to share the climb with you to enable you to regularly save to achieve this specific dream. The dream may involve extra time off work so you may need to get your employer involved. You now have two lists of possible fellow climbers next to 3 dreams. Narrow this down by now choosing 1 of your 3 dreams that you wish to start planning towards achieving. Now you have your dream and fellow climbers chosen, spend some time thinking of the best approach to each of your fellow possible climbers on your lists to get them on board with your climb to provide the necessary support? How you approach these fellow climbers is very important to getting them fully on board, to have their full support. Whether you sell the dream to them, the benefits of you fulfilling your dreams to them or just the support required, you know each of these people and should be able to work out the best approach to use. Pray for each of your fellow climbers before you approach them, praying that they will want to join in your climb and that your dream will lead them to dreaming more themselves.

Chapter 5 – Crevasses and False Summits *(Brian Jackson)*

*"**Any achievement begins with a decision;** the decision to commit, to go for it, to be bold enough to go for it whole heartedly and not to downscale your ambitions and dreams at the first bit of negative feedback."* Leon Taylor – "Mentor".

*"**You must give everything to make your life as beautiful as the dreams that live in your imagination.**"* Roman Payne - American novelist and itinerant traveller.

On most mountain climbs, to reach the summit, you will normally need to head down as well as up, trekking down a slope or intersecting valley or traversing on similar contours before climbing up to reach a higher altitude. For example, climbing Chhubohe, we climbed from 840m (2,756ft) to 5,640m (18,504ft), which would seem that we therefore had 4,800m (15,748ft) of height gain. This however was not the case, as with all the descending we had to do on route, 1,350m (4,429ft) of trekking downhill, we needed to ascend 6,150m (20,177ft) to reach the summit. The famous trek to Everest Base Camp from Lukla airport starts at an altitude of 2,860m (9,383ft) and finishes at Base Camp at an altitude of 5,380m (17,651ft). This is an overall height gain of 2,520m (8,268ft). However, in reality there is over 2,000m (6,562ft) of descending so the trek involves more than 5,000m (16,404ft) of ascent on the route to get to Everest Base Camp. The larger and higher the mountain, often the more downward slopes, tricky cliffs, false summits and even crevasses you will need to cross before getting to the summit. This can be the same with our dreams. The more complicated and bigger the dream is, the more potential obstacles there are on route to achieve the dream. These obstacles to summiting can be both internal and external. Internal obstacles can include our own doubts, fear of failure, inability to get started, poor motivation, whereas external obstacles can include inadequate finance, insufficient time, and lack of support from others.

The external obstacles are mostly practical and can be overcome with practical applications, by appropriate planning. For inadequate finance, think of overtime, extra work, selling unwanted or rarely used items, a regular savings plan; for insufficient time, think of using annual leave, saving up annual leave for one large chunk of time, asking for unpaid leave or taking a gap year; for lack of support, look further outside than your normal network of friends and family, think of work colleagues, join other social clubs to expand your network of friends. I do not mean that any of the external obstacles are to be underestimated but that with a proper plan in place, they can be overcome, given time. This may mean that once you have looked at the obstacles facing you and drawn up a plan to overcome them, your dream now moves from challenging to moderate, or tough to challenging and enables you to complete the plan necessary to fulfil your dream. We will deal more with the external obstacles in the next chapter "Taking Steps to the Summit". In this chapter I would like to focus on the internal obstacles which are the obstacles that can often be far more difficult to overcome than the external ones. This is because they are an issue of belief, of attitude and of the heart. These doubts and fears can be deep seated and entrenched in us and can also be reinforced by others. It is often those people who have stopped dreaming themselves that can be the most cynical towards our dreams, reinforce our own doubts and therefore become the biggest blockers to our dreams.

"And it will be said: Build up, build up, prepare the road! Remove the obstacles out of the way of my people." Isaiah 57:14.

We need to be careful that we do not fall into this trap ourselves and we should always look to support others in their dreams whenever the opportunity arises. A few years ago, one evening as I was sat at home eating dinner with my wife, Steph, she put forward the idea of her doing a Masters Degree as something that she thought would be beneficial to her career. I, without thinking, immediately brought up a list of obstacles to this idea which involved finance, time and the effort involved. I was being a dream blocker and was reinforcing some of Steph's own doubts and fears. It was only later that same evening when preparing for bed that I realised what I had done and how damaging my reply had been to my wife's dreams. I needed to be a supporter, a facilitator of dreams, a fellow climber, not a blocker. I apologised to Steph and we sat down to discuss ways of managing the time issues and any other obstacles that could be in the way. We drew up a plan for overcoming the obstacles, and set a timeline for when the dream would start. Let me allow Steph to tell this story from her point of view:

"No one likes to be told that they can't do something so when I shared with Brian that I wanted to study for my

Masters and he told me all the reasons why it wouldn't work, I was hugely disappointed. The negativity impacted me in two ways. Firstly, on a professional point I needed the MSc to progress in my nursing career and the MSc would provide me with the clinical skills to improve. Secondly, personally, I felt that if Brian didn't believe I could do it then I was obviously fooling myself that I had the ability and capability to do it. Yes, I knew it would be tough and involve sacrificing social time but I was prepared to put the hours in and persevere to fulfil my dream. I needed Brian to be 100% behind me on this to be able to fulfil my dream so it was such a huge relief when Brian changed his opinion and started to see how much this dream meant to me personally and professionally. Once we joined together in this, it was so much easier for me to start planning how I could achieve the dream and also how Brian could help me. Fulfilling this dream was hard work and it took me five years to achieve my MSc on a part-time basis. It would have been much harder without Brian's support and encouragement and I firmly believe that I would not have been able to complete the course without him. The fulfilment of my dream was realised on my graduation day when I saw how proud Brian was when I was dressed in my gown and mortar board, collecting my MSc certificate."

So how do we go about removing our doubts and fears?
How do we overcome our internal obstacles to fulfilling our dreams and reaching the summit? Well firstly it is about focus.

What and who are we focusing on? Are we focusing on the obstacles rather than the dream? As a Christian, I ask myself, am I focusing on the obstacles rather than on God *"who can do immeasurably more than all we ask or imagine"* (Ephesians 3:20)?

Let me illustrate this by using a story from the Bible of the spying out of the Promised Land. Moses is told by God to *"send some men to explore the land of Canaan, which I am giving to the Israelites."* God has already said here that He is giving them this land, it is a foregone conclusion, a done deal. They just have to go and see how wonderful the land actually is and report back. The report they bring back goes like this:

*"We went into the land to which you sent us, and it does indeed flow with milk and honey! Here is its fruit **but** the people who live there are powerful, and the cities are fortified and very large. The land we explored devours those living in it. All the people we saw there are of great size. We seemed like grasshoppers in our own eyes, and we looked the same to them."* Numbers 13: 27-28,32-33.

They return and do report about part of the dream of the land itself **but** then turn their focus upon all the obstacles to this dream and their own doubts and fears then grow. The Israelites then go back to the desert and wander for another 40 years rather than "climbing their unclimbed mountain" and living in this amazing land promised to them by God. We need to learn how to change our focus. How do we do this? Often, by completing smaller moderate dreams, this can spur us on and provide us with more self-belief that all our dreams are possible, not just the moderate ones but also the challenging and tough dreams and even the "Everest" dream. It therefore makes sense to start with some of your easier to achieve moderate dreams, set up your plan to fulfil these and then move onto bigger and bolder dreams as each dream is achieved. As you progress through your dreams list, you will become more and more confident, have far less doubt, gain more self-belief and learn to focus on overcoming problems, and planning strategies, rather than focussing on the crevasses in your way.

I recently had the pleasure of meeting a professional mixed martial arts fighter called Aaron Aby. He has certainly overcome many obstacles to get where he is today. Here is his story:

"I was born with Cystic Fibrosis (CF) which can make it hard for me to breathe and for my body to digest food. CF is progressive, mostly affecting the digestive tract and lungs, which become clogged with thick, sticky mucus, leading to tissue damage and is a life threatening and life shortening disease. Having CF has led me to be passionate about my health, nutrition and fitness. My dream as a young boy was to be good at sports and as a school kid growing up I was always into sports and you would see me taking part in any and every sport possible and having fun doing so. I loved the physical activity and the competitiveness it brought as well as helping my body counteract the CF. As I grew into my teens, football became my main sport and I now set my dreams higher to become a professional footballer. I played for Shrewsbury Town for four years and in this time represented Wales at

under 15, 16 and 17s level playing with the likes of Aaron Ramsey, Joe Allen, Gareth Bale and Neil Taylor. My family would support me by travelling around Europe with me to watch me play. The physical exercise combined with the mental benefits of competition and socialising with others helped me grow as a person and become independent with my medication and this was how I dealt with my CF.

When it came to be giving out the full-time football contracts, the club informed me that they were unwilling to take a risk on my health so decided not to offer me a full-time contract. This had been my dream since sports and especially football took over my life. My dream had been crushed, it had been taken away from me because of a disability I was born with. I left the club to a standing ovation from players, parents and coaches and though I was terribly upset I knew I had to bounce back and adjust my dreams. I spoke to Wrexham FC and they allowed me to attend their pre-season training and they then signed me for a one year part time contract. This provided me with both the time and money to go to college and study sport science.

During my time in college, my Uncle Julian Aby started a Mixed Martial-Arts (MMA) class with all proceeds going to the charity, The Cystic Fibrosis Trust. Uncle Julian had travelled the world studying MMA and wanted to combine his interest in MMA with raising funds for CF. It was very natural for me to then start training with him. This started as only once a week, then twice a week and then before I knew it I was asking my Uncle to take me on *my own for extra one to one training. I started picking it up very fast and became addicted to learning about all the different techniques and loved the way it helped me be in control of my body. I was doing this alongside my football and college.*

After one year at Wrexham FC I went to play in the Welsh Premier League but football just wasn't the same for me anymore. My dream had evolved and changed to reflect my newfound passion for MMA. I started competing in MMA and went on to win my first 4 amateur fights and 3 semi-professional fights. I now knew that this was my dream, to become a full time professional MMA fighter. I wanted to dream bigger than before so I decided to dedicate myself to the sport to become the best I could be. To enable me to do this, I needed to find a full-time gym where I could train regularly and after some searching I found the MMA Academy in Liverpool. This then became my second home. I would train here in the days I didn't have university and then back home in Wrexham at night with my Uncle.

I have now grown in the sport and as a person and the active lifestyle and focus on nutrition led to improvements in my health and coping with my CF. I have now fulfilled my dream and am a professional MMA fighter. I train most days of the week and manage my condition carefully.

I finished my degree at Glyndwr University, Wrexham in Sports Coaching and now run the Inspire Performance Centre (IPC) in Gwersyllt, North Wales. This facility has brought me great joy and motivation, as I witness people change their lives for the better and this maintains my motivation. I get to use my coaching degree, train and coach an MMA team along with my Uncle and other coaches and work with the public and professional athletes. I have seen people change their lives in this facility. I now help other people to fulfil their dreams."

This really shows that dreams do sometimes involve hard work, determination and the drive to succeed. Aaron started with the moderate dream of joining in sport to overcome his Cystic Fibrosis, then becoming good at sport, he dared to dream bigger, to become a full time professional footballer. When this did not work, Aaron still dreamt big and did not allow obstacles put in his way to overcome his dreams. His dream of becoming a professional MMA fighter has now been realised and he now helps other people fulfil their dreams at his IPC. Aaron's story was not without obstacles, the most obvious being his Cystic Fibrosis he was born with. There were however other pitfalls and setbacks such as not being signed on a full time football contract but his determination to fulfil his dream of overcoming his Cystic Fibrosis led to him becoming the person he is today. When I met with Aaron, I could see his passion shining through him in his love for his sport and the promoting of other's dreams; he is an inspirational character.

"We all have dreams. But in order to make dreams come into reality, it takes an awful lot of determination, dedication, self-discipline, and effort." Jesse Owens – an Olympic athlete who set three world records and tied another in less than an hour at

the 1935 Big Ten track meet and was called "the greatest 45 minutes ever in sport".

"A dream doesn't become reality through magic; it takes sweat, determination and hard work." Colin Powell - the first African American appointed as the U.S. Secretary of State, and the first to serve on the Joint Chiefs of Staff.

"Champions aren't made in the gym. Champions are made from something they have deep inside them – a desire, a dream, a vision." Muhammad Ali - American professional boxer, generally considered among the greatest heavyweights in the history of the sport.

We have dealt with crevasses (obstacles) on the climb and how to overcome them but what about dealing with false summits. For those of you who may never have heard of a false summit, this is when you think you are nearing the summit to achieving your dream and then it turns out you still have a distance to go to reach the summit. If you have false summits on route to your dream summit, how do you react, what do you do?

I have already written at the start of this book about climbing Chhubohe, a previously unclimbed mountain in Nepal. The following year I decided to fulfil another dream of mine, this time to take others to the summit of an Unclimbed Mountain to experience the same euphoria I had upon summiting Chhubohe. I decided to go back to Nepal with a team of 5 other dreamers to try and climb Nar Phu Peak (5,930m / 19,455ft), another unclimbed mountain. I'll begin the story on summit night at 5am, 3 hours into the climb......

"........I had spent a lot of time using my binoculars from base camp looking for a feasible route through the ice fall and after much frustration and soul searching about a feasible and safe route, had opted for an ice ramp at the glacier's right hand edge. I was now standing at the bottom of this ice ramp at 5am, with the temperature before wind chill of -25°C (-13°F). The wind had been our constant companion since we had set off at 2am. It had taken some effort to reach this point as from our Base Camp we had to traverse downhill losing over 200m of height before climbing upwards to reach the main glacier. We had to climb a 65° ice slope to get onto the glacier and then plod for 2 hours on a slowly rising slope across large crevasses to reach our current position. Standing at the base of the icefall, it seemed a lot steeper now but I knew the group could get up this and it would not stand in the way of our route to the summit if we kept our nerve. The first warming rays of the sun were cresting the Annapurna range of mountains behind us, which would normally have lifted the spirits of the whole team but the wind was not abating as it would normally do at this time of the day, it was actually growing stronger and despite the suns' appearance, the temperature was dropping. I calculated that it was now around -35° C (-31° F) with the increased wind chill. There was a real urgency now within the team to keep moving to increase the blood circulation around our frozen fingers and toes so we did not stop for a break at the base of the icefall but continued straight up the ice ramp. The ice started out at an easy 45° allowing us to plant our ice axe to our side, take two steps forward and then repeat the manoeuvre but the ramp however soon

steepened to 65° hard ice. We now had to front point with our crampons kicking our feet forward for purchase with each step and use both our ice axes to keep climbing upwards. This was exhausting at this altitude, and blowing very hard, took us over 45 minutes to reach the top of the ramp and out onto the higher glacier. We were now without the icefall's protection so felt the full force of the wind. Ice crystals and hard snow were blown into our faces like small tiny daggers but we were in real need of a drink and a snack so had to stop, huddling together on the ice turning our backs to the wind. My water and several others' had now frozen so we spent some time chipping away at the ice in the mouth of our water bottles to get some fluids into our bodies.

As we sat with our backs to the wind, Rhiannon complained that she could not feel her feet. This could be a serious problem and lead to the onset of frostbite so we took off her boots and massaged her feet, placing them into our armpits to re-warm them before helping her fit them back into her boots. It was certainly getting colder and colder.

At this point on the upper glacier, we had an important route choice to make. We could see much more of the route now that we were above the icefall as this area had previously been hidden from our view at Base Camp by the large icefall. Do we continue along the glacier to the col between our mountain and a climbed one to the West, another kilometre of ice with several large open crevasses to cross and then climb the West Ridge, or, do we attempt to climb directly on the West Face where we are currently standing at the base? After a quick discussion with the Sherpas, we made the decision to take the safer and quicker, but much steeper route straight up the West Face of Nar Phu Peak.

We were now in a fight against the elements as the wind speed really picked up, throwing more snow and ice into our faces, freezing exposed skin and even our hands through our double gloves and making communication between the team members almost impossible; we were only 5m away from each other as we moved together on our safety rope.

The West Face was very steep with snow pitches of between 50°-75° that meant either front pointing or side steeping up the face. This was extremely tiring climbing, as the higher we climbed, the poorer the snow quality became, taking two steps forward only to fall through powder snow and move back one step or even sliding past where we started from. When we slipped, we were constantly pulling on the person on the rope above us and being pulled on by the person behind us when they slipped. This frustrated all the climbers and increased the difficulty in placing your feet correctly to avoid slipping.

As we climbed the face, we could see the top of the slope and the "summit". It took us a further numbing 2 hours of climbing to reach the small plateau and it was only when we reached it, crawling over the top that we realised this was a false summit and the real summit was still 150m above us. Our energy levels were now low, we were tired, *extremely cold, and mentally exhausted. Not only were we not on the summit but the most difficult and dangerous section was still before us with a large crevasse to cross and a very steep 80° ice and snow wall blocking our route. I was feeling shattered and more than a bit negative about our chances of summiting as the time was racing away and I knew that we could now be descending the steep West Face in the dark. We gathered close together on this small false summit of snow so that we could talk with each other and Sherpa Pasang suggested that this was our summit today, the highest point we would reach and we should now turn around. I could see the dejection on the faces of all the team as he said this and I was sure this was mirrored in my face. To have climbed this far not to reach the top was heart breaking. Should we stop here, as descending in the dark would be tricky? Could we really call this completing our dream? Was I denying the group and myself our dreams if I now agreed to turn around 150m below the real summit? I was faced with a really difficult and important decision to have to make so I talked to Pasang alone for a moment to rethink the situation. I wanted so much to push on to achieve the dreams of the whole team of climbing this unclimbed mountain and would use all my strength and determination to keep us moving upwards. We decided that we could descend safely in the dark back to Base Camp as long as we got down to the glacier in the light so we agreed to go for the summit and see if we could make it in the time we have left before needing to turn around. Pasang and I set a goal of 2pm to reach the summit or have to turn around and descend. We kept this* deadline to ourselves but informed the group that we were going to go for the summit and emphasised that we must really push on to descend the face before dark. Dorje, one of our climbing Sherpas, crossed the crevasse on a snow bridge and led up the ice wall placing a fixed line, a rope attached to the Face with ice anchors and snow stakes that we either clip into with jumars or hold onto with our hands for more purchase. This allowed us a short break to regroup as a team, to get our strength back and to attempt to get some food and drink inside us. It was now 12.30pm, and we had been on the go since 2am and had only eaten one snack bar and drunk a half litre of water each. I say attempted to get food and drink inside us as the snack bars were now like bars of granite that needed to be warmed, sucked and then swallowed in little pieces after breaking them up with our ice axes. The water was not much better as it was frozen solid in our bottles and we needed to share out water from our remaining flasks.

We each followed Dorje over the crevasse on the snow bridge, scrambling up the face and then crawled the last few metres on our hands and knees to reach the top of the snow wall, exhausted with our efforts at this altitude of 5,900m (19,357ft). There was now only a steady slope of 50° to reach the true summit. I now knew we were going to make it as a complete team of 6 out of 6 and I started crying out of pure joy and emotional relief, my emotions getting the better of me before I even reached the summit. Through the tears, I watched each member of the team *reach the summit and achieve their dream with looks of complete exhaustion, joy, relief, disbelief, and wonder.*

We had reached the rock tower summit on the top of Nar Phu Peak at 10 minutes before 2pm and checking our GPS, we got a reading of 5,930m (19,455ft). We had done it, we had climbed an unclimbed peak, and we were the first summiteers of this mountain. To stand where no one had previously stood in the history of humanity was exhilarating and emotional! We had achieved our dreams!"

Writing this and reliving the emotions, I know that we could very easily have turned around at the false summit and would have rationalised why it was the correct and safe decision to take under the circumstances. We had been on the go for almost 11 hours at this point and still had to descend so the temptation to turn around was most definitely there. It took a real drive and lots of hard work to keep going; to push forward for the dream. The decision to continue was actually made easier because I had fellow climbers invested in the dream alongside me. It was not just my dream to not complete but other's dreams also. The drive and determination came from wanting others to succeed as well as myself, to overcome the false summit, to push on and find my limits. This is often the case with tough dreams. The nature of many tough dreams naturally leads to several false summits and crevasses on route. I think by previously achieving other dreams by overcoming crevasses and false summits, I already had the skills in place and knew how to push on and I knew that the satisfaction I would feel by completing it would far outweigh any other issues I had at that present moment. I was much closer to the main summit, to the fulfilment of my and other's dreams at the false summit than I would be if I had to start over from Base Camp once again the next day. That is of course very easy to see in hindsight but I have seen people give up on a marathon only 2 miles from the end after 24 miles of running and people turn around only 3 hours from the summit of a mountain after 6 days of climbing. Sitting on the false summit of Nar Phu Peak, I needed to take a short break to regroup and think about where we were and what the implications of giving up at this point would really mean. This very short time aside was incredibly useful and allowed me to see the dream in perspective of just another hour or two of pain and climbing to achieve a life-long dream of mine and others in the team. I also had 5 other fellow climbers who were determined to achieve their dream and knew that as a team we were very strong together. All the moderate dreams that I had achieved in the past provided me with a belief that I could achieve this much larger tougher dream. **Never underestimate the power of fulfilling smaller moderate dreams; they can equip you with the necessary determination, perseverance, belief, and drive to achieve your challenging and tough dreams.**

Christopher Reeve, the American Actor famous for playing Superman once said, *"At first, dreams seem impossible, then improbable, then inevitable"*. He said this, not when he was at the height of his acting career, but after he was paralysed in an accident in an equestrian competition.

Determination is defined in the dictionary as "firmness of purpose". Therefore the purpose of your dream is one of the most important factors to whether you will have the endurance to continue to pursue the dream when crevasses and false summits arise on route to its completion. Your motivation is the key to shaping your level of determination and drive so important to the achievement of dreams, especially tough dreams that may be harder to achieve.

Hebrews 12:1-2 *Therefore, since we are surrounded by so great a cloud of witnesses, let us also lay aside every weight, and sin which clings so closely, and let us run with endurance the race that is set before us, looking to Jesus, the founder and perfecter of our faith, who for the joy that was set before him endured the cross, despising the shame, and is seated at the right hand of the throne of God.*

1 Corinthians 9:24-27 *Do you not know that those who run in a race all run, but only one receives the prize? Run in such a way that you may win. Everyone who competes in the games exercises self-control in all things. They then do it to receive a perishable wreath, but we, an imperishable.*

God rewards determination so let us become determined in achieving our dreams, relentless in our pursuit of them.

"For many of us, we are programmed to avoid discomfort, which leads us to take the path of least resistance or not stretch ourselves" Leon Taylor – "Mentor".

A young lady, Steph Black, who I recently had the pleasure of trekking with certainly showed determination over a very long period of time to fulfil one of her long held dreams, that of climbing Kilimanjaro. Here is Steph's story:

"*Getting diagnosed with type 1 diabetes in 1998, at the tender age of 8, made for some interesting memories. I was frequently chased around the room with a needle, had sherbet taken away from me, and was told by experts that I couldn't join the army, go on a submarine or be a pilot. It all seemed a bit negative. Fast forward 10 years and I had built up a steely resolve to the stereotype that I was less able to achieve. I had no diabetic complications and was about to go off to University! However, my fight against the stereotype was on shaky ground; my diabetic control was certainly not the best.*

I received a leaflet about challenges to raise money for Diabetes UK; one of these challenges was to climb Kilimanjaro. I signed up having done limited research on the mountain but being convinced this would be the big thing to make me take care of myself. However, three weeks before I was due to fly out to Africa I was told by my diabetic team that it was unsafe for me to complete the challenge. I was devastated, and remained so for a number of years. It quashed my belief that diabetes wouldn't hold me back.

Not long after that I decided to reclaim control. I had spent a long time going to sleep at night feeling guilty that I wasn't doing enough to control my diabetes. I worked hard on setting mini goals that I knew would help. It took years and lots of stumbling blocks, but I kept going, making small improvements, always keeping Kilimanjaro in my mind's eye. I had done a training weekend with Expedition Wise Ltd years before, and was reassured that they had taken other people with diabetes up to the summit of Kilimanjaro.

My physical training was relentless; I walked everywhere, completed the Yorkshire three peaks, competed in a duathlon, did hundreds of cross fit sessions, climbed Snowdon and even achieved a '"mini goal"' of walking 39 miles in one day. I also had the mental challenge of staying strong enough to convince some medical professionals that I was up to it – this was one of the hardest things I did. I had to repeat '"yes me"' to persuade a nurse that '"a diabetic"' would be taking on the challenge. One group of people I didn't have to convince were my friends and family. They were there throughout my journey; cheering me on at the side lines, joining me on training walks and supporting me through all of my moments of self-doubt. I felt ready to do Kilimanjaro by September 2016, both mentally and physically so I booked with Expedition Wise Ltd to climb Kilimanjaro via the Rongai Route.

The whole trip went by in a blur. I had lots of moments during the climb where I couldn't believe I was actually there. I knew it wasn't going to be easy and it definitely wasn't. A few things that surprised me were the amount of dust that got absolutely everywhere and having to use two tampons to stop an hour long nose bleed. It was also colder than I could have imagined! I cried every single day either from exhaustion or from feeling overwhelmed that

I was on Kilimanjaro after all the years of dreaming. The motivational quotes, messages and pictures from my family and friends also caused a few happy tears. I was very aware, despite my almost 20 years of insistence, that my diabetes was something that made life harder and doing things like this even more risky. I had trained for the walking, but I had no way of knowing how the altitude was going to impact on my sugar levels. I had to monitor them continuously, because passing out and going into a coma on a mountain would not have a happy ending. Even being dehydrated or getting sick in this environment posed a huge risk to me. Living with diabetes means you are always more aware of your mortality, but being on Kilimanjaro made it all a bit more real – why didn't I just do Ben Nevis?

I had a serious moment on summit night; retching from nausea and dizzy from the altitude and cold, I thought I would have to turn around. Then I heard Brian's very practical advice on the radio: "Steph, if you don't stop stopping you aren't going to make it". My years of fighting kicked in and I said to a probably quite bemused local leader, Imran: "I've worked 8 years for this; I am getting to the top". One more stop to throw up and I made it to Gilman's point, then on to Uhuru peak, and cried my eyes out (until my tears froze and I became too dehydrated to produce more).

I think it's safe to say that some things can make achieving your dreams a bit harder, but with a bit (8 years) of hard work (and tears, exhaustion, and vomiting) and support from loved ones - you can do anything (apart from eat unlimited sherbet, be a pilot, join the army, or go in a submarine). Now for the next challenge…."

Steph showed huge determination in following her dream of climbing Kilimanjaro and this was over a period of 8 years! Determination will allow you to achieve your goals and take hold of all opportunities along the climb. If you do not show "firmness of purpose", you may well suffer from missed opportunities. This can be a real psychological obstacle to achieving future dreams. The main dream that I have shared with you throughout this book is the one I had as an 8 year old boy looking at my first ever photograph in a mountaineering book of Mount Everest and dreaming that I wanted to be the first to climb a mountain in the world just like Sherpa Tenzing Norgay and Sir Edmund Hillary.

I have explained in some detail how as a 38 year-old, this dream came to be achieved. However, this was not the first opportunity I had to fulfil my long held dream. When I was 26 and at University as a mature student, a visiting mountaineer, Daniel Mazur, was speaking at the university mountaineering club that I was involved with and I met with him after the talk. Upon chatting, I was offered a rare opportunity to join an expedition to climb an unclimbed mountain in China. An expedition led by Daniel Mazur was to climb Gasherbrum IV from the Chinese side and also to climb 2 unclimbed 6,000m (19,685ft) peaks to acclimatise beforehand. I would only have been on the expedition to assist but would have had a shot at the lower 6,000m (19,685ft) unclimbed peaks if I proved myself on the trek in to Base Camp. The financial cost was extremely high for me as a student but I even managed to get a hugely reduced return flight offer from British Airways to China. However, in the end, I made my excuses and provided myself with obstacles as to why I should not or could not join the expedition and achieve my long held dream; I did not have the money and it would put me in debt; it would adversely affect my degree; I was too inexperienced to go on the expedition; I was not good enough to climb with the others already booked on the expedition. I wrote down a list of all these and many other excuses, or obstacles to justify why I should not join the expedition to China. The real reason however that I did not join the expedition was none of these very sensible and thoroughly thought through obstacles but the *fear of failure*. I doubted myself that I could achieve my dream and therefore was scared to even try.

Suzy Kassem, an American artist, writer, filmmaker, philosopher, cultural critic, essayist, and poet wrote **"Doubt kills more dreams then failure ever will."**

I had held this dream inside me for 18 years but was not competent at declaring my dreams and achieving them. I had achieved some of my dreams in the past but I would have changed the language to say I had achieved some of my dreams but then some of them were just luck or being in the right place at the right time. I had not really created a culture of achieving dreams, of climbing my unclimbed mountains. This is one of the main reasons behind me becoming involved with writing this book with Nick – to not have others fall into this same malaise, to not have others think they cannot dream or be afraid to dream because of failure. I was prompted to co-write this book to promote the dream achievement culture in every reader, to enable and empower each person to firstly dream, then to achieve their dreams and then to move on to even bigger dreams, and then to support others in their dreams and to pass these skills on, inspiring others and creating a bush fire effect. Dreams are that powerful! After turning down the offer of going to China to climb an unclimbed mountain, it was to be a further 20 years of waiting before I had another opportunity to achieve that dream I had as an 8 year old. This time I took it. Don't wait as long as I did but take the opportunities that are given to you.

What about when we actually fail, or look as though we are going to fail or think we are failing, what do we do then? I would like to illustrate this by going all the way back to a dream I shared with you in Chapter 4, that of losing weight. If you remember, I was on a 3 month programme to lose 10 kilos (22 pounds, 1.5 stones) but did not tell you how much I actually lost over that time period. Well, let me tell you how it went:

I decided to keep a chart for my weight each week to keep me motivated and to measure my progress. The first 3 weeks went really well with my weight dropping by one kilo (2.2 pounds) each week so I was right on target and quite happy with all the effort I was putting in with regards my exercise regime and the protein shakes I was drinking as food replacements for 2 meals per day. Remember that I was doing this over the Christmas period, not the best time to try and lose weight! On week 4, my weight stayed at 77 kilos and then the same on week 5 and then again on week 6, and then onto week 7, I actually gained weight and went back up to 78 kilos. I could not quite believe it as I was following the programme and exercising hard but I was now not only not losing weight but putting it back on. I was disheartened and sat down to think through my options. I came up with 3 main options that were open to me. I would like to share these with you so that you can work out how to achieve your dreams and succeed even in the face of perceived failure.

The 3 main options that are open to you if you are failing to fulfil your plan of action to achieve your dream can be summed up by the three letters, A, C and T. We shall call this the need to **"ACT"** now with the letters A, C and T providing us with the 3 options that are available:

- Option 1 - **A**bandon the dream
- Option 2 - **C**hange the parameters of the dream
- Option 3 - **T**weak the plan but still fulfil the original dream

For my specific dream of losing weight, using the A.C.T. now options, this equated to the following:

- Option 1 – Give up on losing weight
- Option 2 - Lose less weight, or lose a specified number of centimetres off my waist line, or change my body shape
- Option 3 - Lose 10 kilos but lengthen the time necessary to lose the weight, possibly to 6 months

There is the possibility of a 4th option, that of pushing even harder and continuing to try to complete the plan within the original parameters to then achieve the goal. This could be seen to be persevering, demonstrating determination and something to applaud. Our first option when faced with failure should always be to see if this is possible, that with more effort, more finance, more resources, that the original plan is still achievable. Let us not give up too easily or look to change the parameters of the plan if the plan gets too hard, but first show determination. However there comes a time when we know we are at the stage where we have failed already or definitely know we are going to fail, it is worth using the A.C.T. now options to evaluate how to proceed.

Fortunately, for me, at the start of my weight loss, I had taken chest, waist and hip measurements of my body to allow me to check at the end of the diet what the difference would be. I decided to check the measurements now at week 7 to see if this would give me any insight into what was happening. I was astonished to find that I had lost 4 cm off my waist. I realised that with the increased exercise, I was doing gym training 3-4 times per week and this consisted of 30 minutes on the cross trainer but also crucially, 30 minutes on weights, the weights I was doing along with the increased protein intake in my diet was contributing to a build-up of muscle which was why I had reached a plateau in my weight and actually then increased one kilo between week 6 and week 7. Upon realising this, I was able to revisit my dream of losing weight and think about the real reason I had written that down as a dream. Was it really about weight or was it that I wanted to get rid of my belly and look and feel better? I realised that the weight was not the be all and end all of my dream but that it was a vehicle to my real dream of looking and feeling better about my body. I had already discounted working harder, faster etc as I saw this original dream was unfeasible in the time frame I had set myself so was now able to look at the 3 possible options open to me, A, C & T and choose which one was appropriate for me at this time. I immediately discounted option 1, to abandon the dream altogether as I still wanted to sort out my body. I therefore decided to use a combination of both options 2 and 3. I would choose option 2, to change the parameters of the dream, to have a better-looking body by reducing my waist line by 8cms and I would choose option 3, to change the parameters, to lengthen the time of the plan to still fulfil the original dream to lose 10 kilos but over an extended period of 6 months.

After 5 months, I have lost 8cms off my waist and have lost 9 kilogrammes, so I am well on the way to fulfilling my dream. Most importantly I have moved from a maturation age of 56 to one of 42 and I am now 49 years of age.

Dreams can evolve over time so do not be afraid to revisit them, to tweak them or change the parameters to fit your circumstances and current situation.

"Sometimes on the way to your dream, you get lost and find a better one." Lisa Hammond – Permission to Dream: Stepping Stones to Create a Life of Passion and Purpose.

It may be that you have set yourself a goal of saving a certain amount of money to fulfil a dream within 6 months but a financial crisis comes along to rob you of those savings. Rather than abandon the dream altogether, think about changing the time scale. Alternatively, it may be that you have a financial windfall and are able to reach your savings target much sooner than the original plan. Move the plan forward and push on to fulfil your dream even earlier than planned. We need to continually adapt to changes in our circumstances and review the plans to fulfil each dream.

To provide another example, after the success of the Unclimbed Peak expedition in 2014 to Nar Phu Peak with 5 clients, I decided to have an even bigger dream of leading a group of a minimum of 10 people to reach the summit of an unclimbed mountain in Nepal in 2015. By February 2015, we had recruited a group of 11 people who were all excited about climbing Raungsiyar, an unclimbed mountain in the Rolwaling valley of Nepal. We had all the logistics in place and had completed a training weekend together ramping up the anticipation and excitement of the upcoming expedition in November of the same year. However, disaster was to strike in Nepal with two huge earthquakes in April 2015 that devastated the country and put all our plans on hold as we discussed whether it was even morally right to go to Nepal later in the same year on a 'holiday' walking past the actual region of the second earthquake. We decided to postpone the dream of climbing an unclimbed peak and to also change the fundraising we were doing to now raise money for Shelter Box Nepal. Then, in early November 2015, 3 local Sherpas from the Rolwaling valley decided to climb 3 unclimbed peaks in their valley to highlight the beauty of the valley, the opportunities of climbing unclimbed peaks, and to inform people that it was safe to come back to Nepal. One of these peaks was Raungsiyar with another being Langdak, our back up peak. Now we had to not only change the time frame of the plan to fulfil our dream but find a new peak. We did some research and found another possible peak, Jabou Ri, which was promoted to the group to climb in November 2016. Late in November 2015, two British climbers climbed Jabou Ri, further frustrating the possibility of our fulfilling our dream. At this point, with the number of unclimbed peaks quickly disappearing and the ones left being too difficult for our group to climb, I was thinking about the possibility of completely abandoning the dream altogether. However, I realised that this was now not only my dream but that of 11 other people who were invested in this dream. After a lot of work and research, I eventually found a possible alternative peak that was more technical and 200m higher at 6,326m (20.754ft), but still possible. This seemed to be the answer and we now had 14 of us ready to climb our new Unclimbed Peak. In the intervening months in April 2016, I went on a challenge with one friend to climb a more technical unclimbed mountain that lay in the same valley as our group's new goal for November 2016. The weather was appalling and we didn't make it even to the summit slopes but we did have time to recce the route for the new peak for our large group. We soon realised that it was nigh on impossible for our group of "trekkers" as it was a technical rock climbing peak that had not been very clear on Google Earth when we researched it. We did however find a peak right adjacent to it that was unclimbed and perfect for the group at about 6,000m (19,685ft) with a high glacier camp and lots of glacier work and steep summit slopes to climb. Once again, our objective had changed and been tweaked, the parameters had changed but the overall dream was still the same, to climb an unclimbed peak with a large group. At the point of writing this, I have recently returned from a successful summit attempt of that peak, which we called Karbu Ri (White

Peak in Tibetan) at 6,010m (19,718ft). In all, a team of 4 climbing Sherpas and I led a team of 10 to the summit, all fulfilling dreams of climbing a previously unclimbed peak.

"The greatest glory in living lies not in never falling, but in rising every time we fall." Nelson Mandela –   First black President of South Africa, written after his 27 years spent in prison on Robben Island.

  Put another way, fulfilling dreams lies not in never failing to achieve, but achieving even after every time we fail. To illustrate this, I would like to introduce you to Jojo whom I met whilst we were writing this book and looking at avenues to promote it. She is an amazing lady and I will leave her to tell you just part of her story which really demonstrates getting up again and again and showing real determination:

"I was admitted to Birmingham QE Hospital on the 12th of November 2014. This was a real blow as it was the day before my 39th birthday. As a mother of 5, being separated from my children for frequent hospital visits was not unheard of and I have lost count of how many times I have been rushed into hospital, but still each time seems to get harder being away from my children.

I have a condition called Ehlers Danlos Syndrome (EDS), a rare and incurable disease. The obvious thing about EDS is pain, "double jointed-ness" loose joints, fragile skin resulting in scars, bruises, fatigue, dizziness and an array of heart and blood pressure problems. The collagen is lacking within my genetic makeup, making vessels, organs, bones and skin extraordinarily bendy, soft and susceptible to ruptures. Growing up with this condition and permanently being in splints, damaging myself and feeling very unwell, you become acquired to this way of living. This becomes your "normal". It's quite odd, because when I felt well, I knew something was wrong.

Not on this occasion. This admission to hospital was completely different to anything before.

In January of 2014, I fell down the stairs at my house due to fainting after a very important mummy pampering session, (a hot bath!). This is my place to lay back, relax and brush off the pains and aches of the day, re-charging and focusing on the next day's routine and trials. After much reasoning and talking myself into conversations I needed to have, bills I needed to pay and emails I needed to respond to, I decided enough was enough and the chores were outweighing the relaxation time. Reaching over the bath I grabbed my towel whilst standing up very quickly. I could feel my insides shaking and I wanted out of the steamy bathroom quickly. I opened the door and the hit of cold air was refreshing. I thought I was alright, but then as I stood at the top of a very steep and wooden stairs, I collapsed. I don't remember the fall, I don't remember the thud, the clank, or even how my ankle went through the bannister railings backwards.

Upon coming around, I felt the devastation, I had dislocated my hip, ankle, shoulder and my elbow was doing weird things; this was going to be a painful one. I tried to call out to Debbie, a live-in carer, but I could barely breathe. It hurt everywhere, in fact I felt dreadful, I felt so ill that when Deb looked at me she called an ambulance immediately. I was blue lighted to the nearest hospital.

It transpired that I had fractured my back, my ankle had dislocated, my hips had both dislocated and my elbow had sub luxated. As you can imagine, the bruising was like a colour chart of blues and greens with subtle tones of pinks, reds and infused yellows. This incident happened in late January so the road ahead was going to be a long one.

A wheel chair was provided to help me get about as I had my arm in a sling and my ankle was well bandaged. Time suddenly felt like it was going in slow motion.

My fiancé, Nathan, was brilliant in making me feel that a wheelchair was normal and it had to be done. There was never any moaning or complaining that he had push me around or huffing and puffing in unfolding it out of the car or packing it back into the car; he just got on with what was there in front of him.

People who know me know I am not one who likes to sit down. I am someone that despite pain and frequent dislocations, will carry on. This time it was so severe that even I knew I couldn't. There was a difference. I was reliant upon Nathan. I was dependent on his strength and love to get me from A to B. Being in a wheel chair was very frustrating but somehow was also very humbling.... I now had an idea how the public looked upon people in wheelchairs, and that sadly, is very condescending. I overheard one lady look at her boyfriend and say, "she is too pretty to be in a wheelchair" to which I replied loudly back "you look too pretty to be walking". Once in a supermarket, we had so much fun, there was a youngish man in a wheelchair with a broken leg and his wife was pushing him around, Nathan and I looked at each other and looked over to them and shouted, "Race you". With a wink from the opposition the race was on…. it was hilarious; wheelchairs screeching through the aisles, me egging Nathan to go faster, the other couple screaming with laughter at this unforeseen event but a much welcomed one at that. The other customers were cheering us on and laughing hard. Some of the customers were taken aback but I just sweetly smiled and said who would have thought someone in a wheelchair could have so much fun. Nathan helped me more than I realised and with his non-moving, non-wavering, strength he encouraged me to push through and accept that I was in a wheelchair. This was a blessing but also a curse. I wanted to do better than his acceptance, I wanted to prove that it wasn't going to be like this forever. Our children needed me, I was supposed to be walking, and at least guiding and ushering them around – driving them to their schools, colleges and meeting their friends, this is what Mums did. I was also heavily reliant on Debbie the live-in carer and friend. This is where Nathan and Debbie had to work together to cover everything from school runs, shopping, lifts, hospital appointments and menial journeys just for journeys sakes. I suddenly felt like a failure; I felt isolated and very, very low. I could not do anything myself and had lost all my independence.

Poor Nathan would sometimes go to work and I would send him messages about not being able to do life anymore. I sincerely couldn't. I was scared, in pain, dizzy; subluxations and dislocations were happening an awful lot and even moving from my bed to the toilet I would be violently sick just from the motion. It was looking bleak. I know I sought God, I know He heard me but I couldn't understand why it had to be like this. I remember the verses that God gave me, "I have plans for you – plans to prosper you and not to harm you". This was a strong verse that kept me sustained momentarily. The other verse, "Be still and know I am God" was also comforting – but I was "still". I couldn't move. Something had to change.

Nathan always brought me something to offer relief from the boredom – whether it was flowers, books or magazines. On one occasion, he got some wedding magazines ... to which I cheered up dramatically. This gave me HOPE and I said to him that my dream was to be able to walk to him without any chair or aids at our wedding. This was my reason to banish my low mindset and conjure up as much determination as possible to get out of my wheelchair. A vision, a desire, a dream!

After months of physiotherapy and after seeking advice from consultants and GP's reassuring me that I was healing nicely and was ready to be walking again – I knew I had to live up to that belief. My walking commenced but at a stupidly silly rate, NOT in moderation. I was a fighter and was going to live up to that image. I shuffled, I wrestled with the stairs, I walked, I walked and then walked some more. I had been wheelchair bound for 9 months, so now I was free, I was ecstatic.

Debbie however was concerned and looked at me, boldly stating "I think you are over doing it Jojo. I don't want you to keep on going, please take it steady and know that you are doing brilliantly but stop putting so much pressure on yourself, I don't want you ending up falling again". I fobbed this off persistently, despite what I now know to be sound advice.

A few weeks later it became apparent that I was not wonder woman, neither did I have super hero powers. I was a mere mortal who only dreamed and fantasised of what it would be like to self-heal, to be able to wow the doctors with my ability to fly through my recovery. But alas, I had not listened to good advice and was now paying for it.

November 12th - I was sent to the neuro ward at the local hospital and lay there scared, alone and feeling like I was dying. I closed my eyes wondering if this was it. If I had not lived a good enough life, if my dream of marriage to the man I loved was so offensive to God, had I done something to deserve this set back? For a week, I had not been able to stand without swaying wildly to the left or right, without collapsing, or having an onset of a horrendous headache, accompanied by violent shaking and the most horrendous fatigue. Passing out was occurring maybe 2 to 3 times daily and I knew something was seriously wrong. I couldn't think straight; I couldn't hear properly that I had relapsed. I had no capacity to *think, my brain was lacking in oxygen, causing me to be incompetent to do even the easiest of tasks. I thought I was having a break down, there was talk of a brain tumour, adrenalin fatigue, Chiari Malformation and other kinds of rare and wonderful tumours. It was more than frightening. I could barely string a sentence together, let alone move from the lying flat position. This was it, I was going to die I. I called all my nearest and dearest and closest friends in. The consultants had not seen anything like this. If I stood up my blood pressure rose sky high, my oxygen levels plummeted and my heart rate went up to 230 beats per minute. If I lay back down everything would resume to normal throwing the doctors into a puzzled despair. I was bed bound for 20 days, wheelchair bound for another 3 months, but I was not giving up. I had a transfusion to top up my haemoglobin, a carrier of oxygen, and guess what? I am now walking, breathing, eating, laughing, dancing and dislocating, all with a smile. I fulfilled my dream and with Nathan by my side. Looking back, I managed to deal with a year of hell and I have come out the other end smiling having fulfilled my dream of being able to walk again."*

To Do: To assist you in overcoming the crevasses and false summits on route to climbing your unclimbed mountain, choose 5 dreams from your list (3 of these should be the dreams you chose in chapter 4) and write down all the obstacles you think may stop you from achieving each of them. Now look at possible ways to overcome these. We will spend more time in the next chapter looking at the practical ways to start taking steps on your climb to the summit of your unclimbed peak.

Chapter 6 – Taking steps to the Summit *(Brian Jackson)*

"A dream becomes a goal when action is taken towards its achievement". Bo Bennett – Motivational speaker, businessman, consultant and author of "Year to Success".

"A goal without a plan is just a wish." Antoine De Saint-Exupery - French writer, poet, aristocrat, and pioneering aviator.

How do we make our dreams a reality, rather than just a wish? How do we capture a dream? A dream remains just that, a dream, until you turn it into a plan. A plan will determine action and action will create momentum. Momentum will bring you results and you will be well on your way to fulfilling your dream. We therefore need to plan to achieve our dreams. By planning, we can break the dream down into its integral parts to bring the dream ever closer. How do we then make a plan to fulfil a dream?

Planning to achieve your dream involves setting goals.

"Goals are dreams we convert to plans and take action to fulfil." Zig Ziglar - American author, salesman, and motivational speaker.

To enable us to set goals we are going to look at breaking the dream down into separate goals that we can check off on our route to the summit of the dream. We will set an overall goal, and then break this down further into sub goals along the climb. This is similar to the cairns (piles of rock) that you see on mountains paths. Sub goals or cairns along the climb have two main purposes. The first is to inform you that you are still heading in the right direction; the second purpose is to inform you of your speed of progress along the climb. I would like to add a further reason for adding cairns (sub goals) to your route and that is to allow you to celebrate mini successes on the climb which will in turn keep you motivated.

Taking small steps along the climb is important and especially so when the dream is in the challenging, tough or 'Everest' section as these tend to take a longer time and involve more processes to achieve. I recently read the book by Ben Fogle and James Cracknell, "The Crossing" about their epic transatlantic rowing adventure as they entered the world renowned race across the Atlantic Ocean. It would be useful to use Ben Fogle's experience in preparing for this race as an example of someone fulfilling their dreams by taking small steps (sub goals) on route to the summit.

Ben describes in the book how he had the dream of entering the transatlantic rowing race but had only ever rowed twice before. Along with all the hundreds of logistical sub goals he had to achieve, he also had to get rowing fit for the race. The issue was that he also had a full timetable of filming work and was scheduled to travel to Namibia for the month before the race. He therefore chose to take a rowing machine with him to the desert country of Namibia and train rowing whilst fulfilling his filming schedule. He writes:

"For a month, I rose at 4am every morning to row for two hours before we began filming, and then again in the evening. I rowed

in the desert, out in the bush, on the beach, in front of elephants, and more often than not in front of dozens of Namibian children" - The Crossing: Conquering the Atlantic in the World's Toughest Rowing Race – James Cracknell and Ben Fogle.

This just shows that if you are determined enough and set the correct goals, you can achieve any dream, even rowing across the Atlantic by training in the desert! If you want to read more, then buy the book; it is very inspiring.

Let us now get back to how to achieve your dreams by first setting goals. For setting goals to achieve your dream, we will use the acronym, SMART, commonly attributed to Peter Drucker's "Management by objectives" concept.   We will use these letters to specify the words Specific, Measurable, Achievable, Relevant, Time-phased (or Timely).

To Do: To complete this chapter, you will need to set aside some specific time. It may be worth choosing a time slot each week or even each day to work through the following steps.

Choose one challenging and one tough dream from your dream list that are important to you. Maybe use the ones you have already been working on in the previous chapters.

Now work through each of the categories of SMART as detailed below for both the two dreams you have chosen. It may take some time to cover each letter of SMART, hence the need to set aside some specific time to complete this chapter.

Remember that once you have gone through this process for two of your dreams, these dreams can develop and evolve over time so all aspects of your SMART goals will also need to develop and evolve. This is a very fluid process and you may need to revisit the process several times for each dream.

Specific –

"If you don't know where you are going, you will end up somewhere else." Yogi Berra - American baseball Player, 18-time All Star and 10-time World Series champion, 3-time winner of the American League Most Valuable Player Award and elected to the Baseball Hall of Fame in 1972.

This is where we need to break down the dream into a specific goal, into something tangible. For example, "I want to lose weight" is a great dream but is not a specific goal, whereas "I want to lose 10 kilos over 12 weeks" is a specific goal and still fulfils the dream of "I want to lose weight". To enable you to make a dream into a specific goal, you should ask yourself the following questions:

The first question is always "Why?"

Why do you want to do this? Why have you chosen this dream? You need to be honest with yourself to see if the dream you have chosen is a priority in your life at this time as it may involve sacrificing other dreams to fulfil this one. It will most likely involve an investment in time, finance, effort, and resources. Your motivation behind your dream is probably the most important element to the successful achievement of your dream. We will look at this in more detail under the letter "R" for Relevance but it is so important that I highlight it at the start of this process as the dream you choose to work into a SMART goal and sub goals should be one that you are extremely motivated to see through to the end, to reach the summit.

<u>The next question is "What?"</u>

What does my dream look like? What is the outcome? Look forward in time to the completion of the dream and ask yourself what will that look like. For example, if your dream is "I want to learn Spanish", where do you wish to be at the end of the dream? Do you want to be fluent, have conversational skills, or be able to get along on Spanish holidays? By determining what your end point is, what your dream will look like, this will help you become more specific about the dream itself and to then write down specific goals to be able to achieve the dream. Continuing with the example of "I want to learn Spanish", does this mean you will need to visit Spain, does it mean that you need to buy a DVD in Spanish (beginners, intermediate and/or advanced) or complete a class in Spanish at your local college? "I want to learn Spanish" could then become the specific goal of "I want to be able to hold a conversation with a person in Spain when on holiday this July". To use other examples, let me share some of the dreams I have come across when talking to people and then change them into specific goals.

- "I want to own a sports car" could become "I want to buy a Mazda MX5 1600 S that is less than 6 years old within the next 18 months"
- "I want to get to know the Bible better" could become "I want to read the Bible in a year programme"

- "I want to get fitter" could become "I want to be able to complete my first sprint triathlon within 12 months".

This last dream of getting fitter is an interesting one as many of us have this dream but may find it hard to break down into a specific goal. You could become very specific and talk about increasing the level of your VO2 max by 20% in 6 months. However most of us are not really interested in this level of specificity but we do have a picture of where we want to be at the end of the dream. To use an event or activity that you would like to take part in can therefore be the end goal, requiring you to then take part in fitness building activities to fulfil the dream.

Predicting the outcome of a dream becomes far more difficult to make specific when the dream is less tangible such as "I want to have a better relationship with my father". To break this down into a specific goal or goals is a much more difficult proposition, but still achievable. You still need to ask the question "What does a better relationship with my father look like?" It may be that it is being able to spend more time with him without arguing, to spend any time together, or to be able to have a civil conversation over the telephone or in person. When you know what you would like the end picture to look like, you can now become more specific in your goal planning. For example, the goal could be "To spend an evening with my father without arguing, within the next year" or "To have regular weekly conversations over the telephone with my father, within 6 months" or "To go away for a weekend with my father, within 2 years".

Another question is "Where?"

Where is this going to take place? For example, if your dream is to become fitter, to make this specific, where are you going to accomplish this? Are you going to join a gym or buy equipment to put in the house or garage? Are you going to run, if so where? If your dream involves travel, specifically where will you travel to? A friend, Phil, shared a dream with me regarding sailing around the Mediterranean. The Med is a big place so I asked him exactly from where and to where is he going to sail? This enabled him to focus more on being specific and to start working out goals to work towards achieving his dream. The more questions he asked himself, the more specific he had to become and the easier it became to write down specific goals to achieve on route to fulfilling his dream to sail around the Mediterranean.

The next question is "How?"

How am I going to do this? How much is it going to cost? How much time do I need to do this? How many other people are affected by my dream and may need to be asked along on the climb? How long will it take? How much effort is this going to require? The "How?" question allows you to break the goal down further into sub goals or cairns on the route to the summit. By asking how, the questions of effort, finance, time, resources, and involving other people are all raised. These questions are extremely important if we wish to achieve our dream, as a lack of any one of these requirements could mean the failure to achieve the dream. Using the dream "I want to learn Spanish", let us look at how we are going to achieve this. We have already made it a specific goal of "I want to be able to hold a conversation with a person in Spain when on holiday this July". We could now break this down further into "I will book onto the beginner's Spanish evening class at my local college which starts in 2 months" and/or "I will buy a beginner's Spanish DVD/CD and set aside each Saturday morning for 2 hours". It may be that you will need to set aside some time to save up the money it costs for the course and to rearrange the time off for the evening classes. This helps to give you some sort of time structure that we will highlight later. From this exercise, you now have your first set of sub goals or cairns to show your progress to your main goal.

- Save up a specific amount of money weekly to meet the evening class fee within 2 months
- Arrange to free up the evening required for the course
- Book onto the course

You already have 3 sub goals or cairns showing you the route and helping to measure your progress to your final goal, to the summit of your dream, of holding a conversation in Spanish when on holiday. If we use another goal to go through the same process, the dream of "I want to get fitter" has become the specific goal of "I want to be able to complete my first sprint triathlon within 12 months". To break this down into sub goals, you could:

- Join a local swimming pool and gym
- Set aside each Saturday morning to go swimming
- Set aside 1 evening per week to cycle (either at the gym on the cycle machine or if the weather is amenable, outside on the road)
- Go running one evening per week

- Talk to someone who has done a triathlon before
- Buy the triathlon kit required
- Book onto the triathlon.

You now have your sub goals and a method of attaining the main goal.

The final question under Specific is "Who?"

Who do I invite along as my fellow climber? Who do I need to talk to for this to happen? Who would be best as my support for this specific dream?

We dealt with the choosing of your fellow climbers in chapter 4 so you may need to revisit this chapter to help you choose your specific fellow climbers.

Example: Dream = "I want to get fitter".
Why = because I want to feel healthier, lose weight, look better and feel more at ease with myself.
What = after 4 months, I would like to be able to enter a triathlon and be fit enough to run the whole challenge without stopping.
Where = book a local triathlon within a 40-minute drive and the swim needs to be in a pool as I am not a confident swimmer in a pool, let alone open water.
How = join the local swimming pool and draw up a weekly training programme. Buy a tri-suit and tri belt. Book the Sprint Triathlon.
Who = get a close friend to join me in the challenge so we can encourage one another and do some training together. Read a few books by unlikely triathletes on tips to keep me motivated.

My "Specific" goal that now comes from the above is = "I will book the Nantwich Cheshire Sprint Triathlon for May 22nd and look to complete the whole course in under 1hr45mins."

To Do: Choose both one of your challenging and one of your tough dreams to break down into goals or steps to the summit. First ask yourself the most important question of why, then the questions of what, where, how and who, for each of these two dreams. You should now have two specific goals combined with the financial, time, resources and effort required for each goal. You should also have a list of people who you need to ask to become your fellow climbers.

Measurable –

"Measure what can be measured, and make measurable what cannot be measured." Galileo – Italian astronomer, physicist, engineer, philosopher, and mathematician who played a major role in the scientific revolution during the Renaissance.

A recent study looked at all the different methods of losing weight including weighing one's self each morning over a period of 3 months. The results were not what you might expect, as the best and most consistent method of losing weight was in fact shown to be the simple task of weighing one's self each morning. Measuring allows us to know we are on the right climb, that we have reached certain markers, it drives us forward, it motivates. We therefore need to be able to measure our goals, their progress, their completion.

How do we know we have fulfilled our dream, achieved the goal, reached the summit if we are unable to measure the goal? To allow us to know this for certain, we need to be able to measure the successful achievement of the goal. Therefore the goal needs to be measurable in some manner. To enable you to measure your progress along the climb and know that you have reached your summit, you should ask yourself the following question:

What will be measured?

Is it time, finance, weight, speed, activity completion? If we go back to the example of "I want to have a better relationship with my father", this is almost impossible to measure but as we have made it a specific goal of "To have regular weekly conversations over the telephone with my father within 6 months", this now becomes very measurable. There is the final summit goal time element of 6 months and the weekly calls. Further measurements could be sub goals of a call within the first month and then fortnightly calls by 4 months. These are measurable and involve a measurement of both the ongoing main element of the goal but also the time involved. The benefits of being able to measure your goals and sub goals (cairns) on route is that they show you your progress and inform you that you are on the right path. Reaching each measurable sub goal also allows you to celebrate each of these achievements along the climb. This becomes even more important for any challenging or tough goals that will necessarily take a longer time to achieve. Therefore, any mini achievements you can celebrate on route help promote determination and stimulate the drive required to succeed. These character traits are so important in the successful achievement of challenging and tough dreams. Rewarding yourself after the successful achievement of each sub goal is also important to maintaining your motivation and hence belief in your ability to achieve the overall goal. Each sub goal is a step on route to the main goal and small seemingly insignificant steps bring you steadily closer to fulfilling your dreams. One of the participants on the recent Unclimbed Peak expedition to climb Karbu Ri used to email me regularly when he had checked off mini-goals on route to this main goal. He emailed me when he bought his double boots, again when he had booked his flight, and again when he had sourced a set of ice axes and crampons. This continued throughout the build-up to the departure and only stopped when we actually flew out to Nepal. He quite often used the phrase "It now seems all the more real and it's getting closer" each time he fulfilled one of his sub-goals (cairns) on route to the main goal (summit). It was great to be able to share these mini triumphs with him at each stage of his climb.

To provide you with another example of this, let us use the dream shared with me by Phil. He had the dream of sailing around the Mediterranean. He went through the specifics of why, how, where, what and who to make the dream more into a goal he could achieve. He then needed to break this down into measurable sub goals. With a tough dream this grand, it needed a lot of breaking down. Here are a few suggestions but this is certainly not exhaustive as each of the following could be further broken down into more steps:

- Approach list of "Who" to have as fellow climbers
- Save up a specific amount of money per month for the Skipper course

- Reach a specific financial target by 9 months for the Skipper course
- Enrol on a skipper course and pay for it
- Pass the Skipper course
- Save up a specific amount of money per month for any needed equipment
- Reach a specific financial target by 5 months for any needed equipment
- Purchase equipment
- Save up annual leave
- Request specific date for holiday
- Research companies to hire yacht from over 2 months and have a list of 3 to choose from
- Choose the yacht hire company
- Save up a specific amount of money per month for the flight, yacht hire and food
- Reach a specific financial target by 12 months for the flight, yacht hire and food
- Book and pay for the flight, yacht hire
- Buy food in country

All these sub goals are measurable and allow you to celebrate your progress towards the final goal.

Example: Dream = "I want to get fitter". I have now set out to complete the Cheshire Sprint triathlon. There are lots of ways to measure my progress to this goal.

I have certain items that I need to buy so I have set aside money to do this – Tri suit, tri laces, tri belt, swim hat, prescription goggles.

I have set a training schedule where I have a minimum of 3 ticks in each box by the end of the week (each activity needs to be a 500m swim, a 5km run or a 20km bike ride).

Week 1	🏊		🚴		🏃	
Week 2	🏊		🚴		🏃	
Week 3	🏊		🚴		🏃	
Week 4	🏊		🚴		🏃	

I have set myself 1 x brick session (2 activities following each other) every other week.

I am reading 2 x triathlon books in the next 8 weeks.

To Do: Using the two dreams you have chosen for the "Specific" section of Goals, now work out how you are going to measure when you have completed each goal. Then break the goals down further into measurable sub goals, cairns on route to the summit, making each measurable in both quantity and time.

Achievable –

"If you think you can do a thing or think you can't do a thing, you're right" Henry Ford – Founder of the Ford Motor Company.

"Don't be afraid of the space between your dreams and reality. If you can dream it, you can make it so." Belva Davis - First African-American woman to become a television reporter on the U.S. West Coast and winner of eight Emmy Awards.

In this section, you will need to ask this simple but very important question, "Is my goal achievable?" As well as asking whether the goal is achievable, you will also need to ask yourself "Am I willing to achieve it?"

As first stated when breaking down a dream into a goal, the most important question is Why? Why is this dream important to you? To consider whether a goal is achievable, the goal will need to be of a high priority, it will need to be important. Therefore, ask yourself the question, is this goal important to me, is it a priority? You will first need to be motivated to succeed as without a strong internal motivation to succeed, there will be no determination and drive to achieve the goals on route to the dream when you face the various obstacles of inadequate or competing time, finance, effort and resources.

To look at whether the goal you have set is achievable, ask yourself the following questions:

- Do I have the time needed to set aside to complete the goal?
- Can I build up the time required to complete the goal?

- Do I have the necessary finances to achieve the goal?
- Can I raise the required finances over time to achieve the goal?

If you need to take longer to raise the necessary finance, this may mean the goal deadline is longer than you first expected. If so, do you have the energy for the long haul?

- Do I have the supporters (fellow climbers) in place to assist me in achieving this goal?
- Do I have the energy and drive needed to complete the goal?
- Does the goal involve other people to be able to achieve it?

The next question is what are you willing to sacrifice, to change or to give up achieving this goal? To prioritise one goal, to make this goal achievable, you may need to put aside other goals for the time being. You may need to adjust finances, energy, time, and resources to enable this goal to be achievable. The dreams that are the most important to you will always rise to the fore and become your motivating force to break down into achievable goals. How many people do you know who have picked up a language book or CD to learn a new language but have not actually achieved learning the new language? Is this because it is not a dream? Is it because learning the language is not achievable? The answer to both of these questions is probably no. Why then have they not been successful? It is most likely that the goal fell by the wayside because other priorities took over the time needed to complete this goal. When other dreams and goals became more important, the effort required to achieve the initial goal is lost. We all have limited time, energy, finance and resources and will only apply these to a goal that is a high priority so when other goals interfere that are perceived as a higher priority, we stop putting any effort into the lower priority goal, leaving the goal unachieved.

To know whether a goal is achievable, you also need to ask the questions:

- Does the goal fit my abilities?
- Do I need to learn new skills or acquire new abilities to enable me to achieve my goal?

The answer may well be that the goal does not fit your abilities now but that does not mean that the goal is unachievable as you may need to gain new skills and abilities along the way to achieving the goal. Remember Phil, whose goal was to sail around the Mediterranean? He did not have the abilities or skills required to achieve his goal so set as part of his sub goals, to attend a training course to become qualified as a Skipper. Asking yourself the question, "Does the goal fit my current abilities or skill set?" will provide you with further sub goals (cairns on route) that you need to achieve to then make your main goal achievable. Don't let your lack of skills and abilities at any time be a hindrance to you achieving your goals.

Some goals do appear to be unachievable but be aware that by breaking the main goal down into sub goals, a seemingly unachievable goal suddenly becomes lots of moderate goals that are achievable.

"Nothing is particularly hard if you divide it into small jobs."
Henry Ford.

If a dream is in your heart as a burning desire and you have the drive and passion to succeed, nearly anything is possible. Miracles happen, God is bigger than you can imagine, and faith is required.

Consider the following person, Sue, whom I recently met whilst talking about dreams: A married lady with three children who works along with her husband training international young people within the UK, but on a low wage. Her dream is to visit every country in the world. Is this dream achievable? At first glance, maybe it does not look as though it is. However, she could go through the process of making the dream into a specific goal of "I want to travel to each country in the world that I have not yet visited over the next 20 years". She could further break the goal down into the sub goals of separate lists of countries she has not yet visited that are near each other so can be visited together and provide a possible time frame to these sub goals. Do you now think this is an achievable goal? Under the current circumstances of her life, this would still appear impossible and an unachievable goal with regards time, and most importantly finance. However, what if the organisation she works for calls her and her husband into the main office one day and informs them both about how impressed they are with all the training the couple are doing in the UK, and because of their success, now wish to roll this training out and expand it to all their international bases. They are aware that this will mean a huge change in the family's lifestyle and they will need to move their whole family every 6 months to a year to a different country. Now, is the goal so unachievable? Who knows what is around the corner, what will happen next? Don't give up on your dreams just because they appear unachievable.

"Start doing what's necessary; then do what's possible; and suddenly you are doing the impossible." Saint Francis of Assisi – Founder of the Franciscan Order.

You need to truly believe that nothing is impossible so that when you come across the impossible, you will find a way around, over, under or through it. This may involve more time, more finance, greater creativity, more help or just a change of perspective, but if you believe it is possible, you will always find a way to fulfil your dreams. If you believe a dream is impossible, you will never invest effort in trying to achieve it. Unbelief results in inaction, whereas belief results in action.

To illustrate this, let me introduce you to Heather and you can see from her story how achievable goals can be even when they seem to be impossible:

"Who you are is defined by the values you are willing to struggle for. And for me, that has been a core concept in my life's journey. I became a Christian when I was seventeen, and when I look back over the course of my life, I realise now that Jesus was always talking to me about His compassion for people and nations. I am a slow learner and He has needed years to help me understand even just a tiny aspect of what love looks and feels like. But it is the greatest adventure...

During my twenties and thirties, when in prayer, I would often find Him showing me pictures (in my imagination) of specific issues that affect nations, such as alcoholism in Alaska, for instance. I am, of course, not naturally compassionate, and I would find these pictures quite bewildering and often disturbing, because I felt so helpless- and uncaring! Alaskans? I didn't know anyone there and had no idea why God would be showing me pictures of them. I would sometimes ask Jesus why He was showing me these things and He would often reply with, 'I just want you to see and experience that this is my heart towards these people. That's all.' Sometimes He would say that He wanted me to pray about what He had shown me- but often it was just that He wanted me to know how He felt about a group of people and what He wanted to do in their lives to bring healing or restoration.

Because of these experiences, I found myself often thinking about world affairs and God's role in them. A passion and desire to see God bring restoration and healing to people in other nations was growing in me, mostly imperceptibly; I am not sure I really realised it was even happening. When I had the opportunity to travel, I would take it! I did a lot of traveling in the UK, helping church groups with conferences and teaching seminars, and had the opportunity to go on small, short-term mission trips to South Africa, Kenya, Uganda and India.

I also asked Jesus how I could be a blessing to foreigners in my home town and in faith, looked around for opportunities and it didn't take long to find some. I am a high school teacher by profession, and I found myself naturally gravitating towards helping Thai and Portuguese students in my classes with learning English and sorting out issues regarding bullying, etc. I decided one day to take in a Thai lady as a lodger, who worked at the local Thai restaurant. It was great fun getting to know her whole family and explore the loveliness of Thai cuisine!

I began to realise the truth of what God had been showing me- that His love and compassion for people everywhere was unstoppable and that His presence and power was available and present for them, just as it was for me. Through all these years, I'd also been praying a very specific prayer, that was almost a compulsion, and I didn't even understand why I had to keep praying this prayer. You may have heard of Ellen MacArthur, a British yachtswoman who has sailed solo around the globe several times, winning many races and overcoming many challenges during those races. My dream was that God would make me like her, in Christian terms. I admired her determination, resilience, bravery and dedication to sailing. I felt Ellen had qualities that I didn't and I desperately wanted to be like her. I grew up as a teenager with some sailing experience, sailing small yachts, so I could appreciate her commitment. I don't really understand why I kept dreaming these things; she had done a great job of sailing round the world and I didn't need to replicate her journey!

In July of 2007, I was part of a small group studying Bill Johnson's book, 'Dreaming with God'. At the start of the year, God had been saying to me, to get ready to go. So, I asked God, "What do you mean? Do you want me to give up my teaching job? Do you want me to sell my house?" The answer to both questions was yes, so I put those things into motion. However, by July, I still didn't know where God wanted me to go and was feeling a bit frustrated. Everyone in the group were facing major transitions, and on one evening, we decided to have some time praying for each other. When it came to my turn to be prayed for, a lady saw a map of the world, with many countries 'glowing', and a long country, further East than Borneo, was glowing more brightly than the rest. My recollection of the geography of that part of the world was hazy and I couldn't think where she might mean at that point. As we were praying, I suddenly began day dreaming about Santa Claus coming down the chimney, which did seem rather random as it was July...and I thought, perhaps that's God's thought, rather than mine, so I explained to the group what I was imagining. Sue, the pastor's wife, screamed and ran into another room, bringing back with her a book wrapped in Christmas paper. She said God had told her to buy it for me last November, and she'd been waiting for the right time to give it to me! The book was one of Ellen MacArthur's: Race Against Time. Wow, nobody knew my dreams about being like Ellen, this was God showing me how He'd been listening very intently to my heart and it was pretty exciting. I wasn't sure what to make of what had happened and then, two weeks later, I received a phone call from some friends in another part of the U.K. asking me whether I'd like to help them crew a 64 foot traditional schooner, sailing from England to the Mediterranean, across the Atlantic to the Caribbean, through Panama, and then across the Pacific, to Papua New Guinea (PNG)....helping with a mission to build boats, give health education and create a Bible School. I said yes, of course, and ran around screaming for a while! Here I was about to fulfil my life-long dream of being used by God and being more like Ellen MacArthur in character.

To fulfil this dream, I had to undertake quite a few tasks to even get started. I had sold my house, given up my teaching job and now spent the remainder of 2007 getting the boat ready, tying up any loose ends and establishing relationships for the next part of this adventure. I also took my RYA coastal skipper course in Gibraltar at the start of 2008 to brush up my sailing skills.

My friends and I sailed down the coast of France and Spain, eventually arriving in Tenerife around May 2008. The sailing was beautiful and difficult, perhaps in equal measure. The twinkling canopy of a trillion stars and a carpet of bioluminescence washing onto the decks in Albufeira was so majestic....and then there was the constant bickering and sniping of my friends on board. Their relationship difficulties skewed everything and we found ourselves just struggling to survive through another day.

Unfortunately, my friends were unable to resolve these problems and the venture fell apart. I spent many hours pacing around the streets of Santa Cruz, praying and wondering what to do. What had happened to my dream? After it was clear that the situation was not going to get better, I returned to Wales, and again, kept praying and still hanging on to my dream. Every time I prayed, God said, 'Go to PNG, Heather.' This didn't make sense to me- I was now in a bit of debt and everything had gone so wrong. My dream appeared to have been dashed and although I had followed all the steps to fulfilling it, the dream appeared to be no closer to being realised than when I had first started dreaming. I decided, well, I could go to PNG and have a look- at least I'd be able to say that I'd gone for a holiday there. I'd have to start again anyway, so what did it matter? And I kept thinking of all that God had done so far- this was His big adventure. It hadn't turned out the way I thought it would, but then maybe that's always the case with big dreams.

In November 2008, I finally got to Papua New Guinea. I went to Alotau, Milne Bay Province, and met a man called Chris Abel, who is the grandson of Charles Abel, one of the first missionaries who came to the area in 1890. Charles established the Kwato Mission on Kwato Island, in the China Straits. As I learnt about Chris and his grandfather's history, I was powerfully impressed by the thought that God was slotting me in to a continuum of His work in this area. I kept meeting Kwato- trained people all through my time in PNG. Chris was excited that God had sent me and we therefore went to ask the Kwato church leadership whether they would like me to come and work with them. I kept praying, kept dreaming and they said 'yes'.

Fantastic! Now, how was I going to afford to finance my dream? I had used most of my finances preparing for the sailing to PNG and now I had an offer to go to work in PNG but did not have the finances. I kept on dreaming and returned to Wales.

Upon my return to Wales I was completely bowled over by the responses of so many in my church family. Independent of any influence from me, many of my friends said that they would support me financially, which meant I could then apply for a visa to return to PNG and my dream was back on track. I applied for my visa at the end of 2009 and travelled to PNG, not sailing this time as would have Ellen Macarthur, but I still fulfilled my dream to work in PNG and ending up staying for two whole years until 2011, working alongside Chris and the section of the Kwato church on Kwato Island and the neighbouring islands. I didn't get to sail to PNG as originally intended but still had an exciting adventure of a lifetime. I was living my dream as an adventurer half way around the world working in PNG. Dreams do not always follow the path you have selected but I have learned never to give up and even the impossible can become possible."

So, the impossible can become possible and even if your dreams need to evolve and change over time, do not give up on them.

Let us now go back to our example of wanting to get fitter.

Example:

- Dream = "I want to get fitter".
- Goal = I will enter the Cheshire Sprint triathlon in 12 weeks and compete it within 105 minutes.
- Sub Goals = I will manage 3 x 20km cycles per week, 3 x 500m swims and 3 x 5km runs per week for 7 of the next 11 weeks (4 weeks overseas).

I now need to ask if this is achievable in the time frame that I have. I am away a lot overseas so to make this achievable, I have set myself a training programme that allows for flexibility. If I cannot get to the swimming pool because I am overseas all week, when I am back home, I can do 60 lengths on a Saturday or Sunday and still have completed 3 x the length of 20m required and I have still got my 3 x ticks against swimming for that week. I have decided to forego the gym and use that time for cycling indoors to still enable me to cover the cycling distance I need but making it easier to do in the busy life that I lead. I am taking my running kit to work and doing a 5km run at lunch time when the weather is good. This means that I do not need to rise earlier, something that will not work for me, or run in the evening which is unachievable as I am always tired by then and not motivated. The training programme I have set myself is therefore achievable and the goal also achievable. I hope to complete the triathlon in 90 minutes so 105 minutes as a specific measurement allows for some give and provides enough motivation to keep training.

To Do: Using the two dreams you have chosen for both the Specific and Measurable section of Goals, now work out if you believe that they are truly achievable. Do you need to change them slightly to make them achievable? Do you need to recruit a fellow climber to make them achievable? Are there other factors that need to be put in place to make the goal achievable for you? Do you foresee any obstacles that will make the goal unachievable and therefore may need to tweak the goals or sub goals slightly? You need to be able to truly believe that the goals are achievable before moving on to the next section.

Relevant –

"The starting point of all achievement is desire". Napoleon Hill - American author in the area of the new thought movement who was one of the earliest producers of the modern genre of personal-success literature.

Your dream needs to be relevant to you, it needs to be a strong desire, a driving force so that you persevere with the dream even when obstacles and frustrations are put in the way of your dream. You need to ask yourself the question; is your dream worthwhile, does it meet your needs, is it relevant to you at this time? Why are you undertaking this dream? Is it important to you to fulfil this dream? Why is it important to you to fulfil this dream?

When looking at your dream list, there may well be dreams on the list that you are interested in but not committed to achieving. This may be because those specific dreams are not relevant to you at this moment in time. To formulate your plan to achieve your dreams, to break them down into relevant goals, you need to have a strong internal desire and commitment to follow through on any goal that is made to achieve your dreams.

"There's a difference between interest and commitment. When you're interested in doing something, you do it only when it's convenient. When you're committed to something, you accept no excuses; only results." Kenneth Blanchard – Author of "The One Minute Manager".

Example: Sprint Triathlon. The desire to get fit, feel healthy and lose weight is top of my immediate list. The kick I needed to put this at the top of my list was the health check and by undertaking 3 different activities, this keeps me from becoming bored and keeps me motivated.

To Do: Spend some time looking at your dreams list and prioritising the dreams as to their importance and relevance to you at this present time.

Time Phased (Timely) –

"Goals are dreams with deadlines." Napoleon Hill

"Never give up on a dream just because of the time it will take to accomplish it. The time will pass anyway." Earl Nightingale - American Radio personality, Writer, respected Speaker and Author.

This can be a critical stage of turning a dream into a goal. We live in a world where most of our time is set for us, whether this be school, college, or work. Therefore to set times and deadlines for your goals to be achieved, you need to be structured, you need to be self-motivated.

How good are you at setting deadlines and sticking to them? You need to be honest with yourself regarding how good you are at fulfilling time deadlines so that when you set out measurements for your goals, they are ones you can reasonably achieve in the specified time.

Some questions to ask yourself when setting your goals:

- When do you want to achieve it by?
- When do you need to achieve it by?
- Are there dynamics within the goal that determine the time required?
- When do you need to start, to finish, to get to certain points along the climb?
- What cairns need to be reached at what times?
- Can you break the goal down into mini bite sized chunks of time?
- Does it all have to be done at the same time?
- Does it have to be achieved over a continuous time or can it be spread over separate sections of time?
- Is it the right time, does it work, is it capable within the time frame, what is the time frame, can this be broken down into even shorter time slots?

All the questions above are very important and should be used to help you break down your dreams into goals. However, I believe that there is a right time for everything, that dreams are fulfilled at the correct time in your life.

"There is a time for everything, and a season for every activity under the heavens." Ecclesiastes 3:1

Heather's story really shows this with her life changing journey to Papua New Guinea but let me illustrate it further by once again using the example of climbing my first Unclimbed Peak. I have already shared with you in the previous chapter that I originally had the opportunity of climbing an unclimbed peak when I was at university at the age of 26 but failed to grab the opportunity at that time. At that point in time, I was fit, young, and I was a good climber on both rock and ice so from an outside perspective, one could say that it was an ideal time for me to fulfil that specific dream, that it was timely. Move forward 20 years and when I finally did fulfil my long-held dream of climbing an unclimbed peak, I was far more mountain savvy, more determined, far better and proven at altitude, more of an experienced mountaineer, and more financially able to undertake the challenge. One could therefore say that at this later point, it was far more "timely". We can never know for sure how things are going to turn out so when you can fulfil a dream, take it and see where it leads you.

"Nothing ever runs completely to plan. It's a rollercoaster at best! That said, it's so important to have plans. How else would you know where you are going? You wouldn't set sail without knowing where you are going and which direction you need to go in order to get there." Leon Taylor, "Mentor".

Example: To get fitter - Sprint Triathlon. The goal is certainly timely as after the health check, I knew I needed to lose weight and get fitter to manage my health better. I have a set deadline to train for which is the Cheshire Sprint Triathlon. I am away overseas for 4 of these weeks. Therefore, my time frame is shortened for training and I need to keep up a certain level. My weekly sub goals as below for 3 x ticks in each box help me check on my progress as climbing past cairns on my route to the summit. Each piece of equipment I buy from my list is another cairn reached on the route to the summit, as is every week I tick off on my wall chart.

To Do: From your previous time of prioritising your dreams under the letter "R" for relevant, choose the most important and relevant to you at this point in time and work through the questions above.

Chapter 7 – The Dangers of not Summiting *(Nick Pengelly)*

"When we give up on our dreams, we die while still alive."
Robin Sharma - Canadian writer, famous speaker, leadership expert and author of 15 global best sellers.

"Hope deferred makes the heart sick, but a desire fulfilled is a tree of life." Proverbs 13:12.

Imagine life, getting up in the morning early, no time for breakfast. A quick drink, into the car, off to work, do a day's work, earn enough money to pay the bills, and plan a bit of a holiday. Home again, eat tea, do a few other jobs before falling asleep in front of the fire. The next day it starts all over again. The weekends consist of a bit more work, a bit more sleep, a few more jobs and time for a few social things. This could be considered a routine life. There is nothing wrong with routine, as we all need to earn money to pay for the basic necessities of life. The issue comes when the routine is all there is and there is no room for dreaming. We all need to dream to avoid stagnation and this gives purpose to the routine.

Imagine for a moment what it must be like if you have trained for months getting into shape, have spent your savings to buy quality mountaineering equipment, have talked so much about this trip of a lifetime that all those around you are now bored of your plans. You have persuaded your nearest and dearest that it is a great use of your savings to buy a plane ticket and book hotels and take all your annual holiday to fulfil the dream of a lifetime and go and climb an unclimbed mountain. To help this trip seem not too self-indulgent, you have also used the opportunity to raise money for a local charity. The scene is set and the trip is on. I am just imagining here as, unlike Brian, I have not even tried climbing on an indoor climbing wall, let alone an unclimbed mountain in Nepal. There are many things that might not work out that are beyond your control. The weather may make the ascent impossible, the snow on the ground, the risk of an avalanche may all mean backing off and not completing your dream. After all the training your fitness is not going to fail you so at least you have that in your favour. As you are making your ascent the conditions seem perfect, all is going well, your local guide is perfect, the team leader knows what they are doing, the world is a good place. As you near the peak other things come into place, a slight mistake results in an injury that stops you continuing or there is the psychological element that you have not accounted for. The altitude sickness hits in and takes over. The mental strength to continue breaks. You hit that point where there is no going forward, there is only going back. The dream is within reach but it is out of reach. Going back down the mountain is not full of smiles and celebration, it is not the story that you have prepared in your head. You need a story that makes you look good but your mind is not able to make one that quickly. A gloom of descent overtakes. The ability to process at this point is vital but it might take time. Will the missed summit become a memorial stone to dreams or will it become a point where you are able to assess and reassess your limits. The dangers of not summiting are there, but the opportunity is the gold that is hidden in the rubble.

You may not of course be climbing a mountain but you might have another missed moment, another missed dream, a failed opportunity. If so, it's time to find the gold so that the hidden dreams can live.

I would like to take a few moments for Ziz to share some of her story, it's not a complete story but an ongoing one. It illustrates the dangers of not summiting but also the opportunities that can still lie ahead.

"As a young child I had a deep conviction (that 'knowing' in the pit of your stomach) that my life purpose was in international social concern and my often unspoken dream was always to be involved, on the ground, with charitable work that is truly combatting poverty and revolutionising lives. Ideally I'd be running my own work, meeting inspiring people all over the world and engaging with the needs of children living in poverty. In my teens I put everything out there, I campaigned for charities, fundraised, volunteered, gave up my Saturdays to volunteer in a charity shop, organised school appeals for Christmas shoeboxes, 'Drop the debt', got familiar with the headmaster's office (in a good way) and was nominated as the 'most likely to change the world by doing good' in my secondary school yearbook. I ran for school council and went to meetings with local politicians and civil servants. I was an idealist, passionate, a fierce believer in change and beautifully naïve. As I left school, I took a gap year and went to a volunteer worker training school. I was the only one in the team to have fundraised the full amount for a year living abroad and had already liaised with the people I'd be joining in Uzbekistan. I was organised and excited and it truly felt that all my dreams were coming true. This was going to be the start for me and every step I had taken led me to exactly where I wanted to be. But of course, as dreams often do, it all went pear-shaped. I didn't go!

I later found out that voluntary workers were being thrown out of the country and visas were being denied. I didn't know that then and I felt completely heartbroken and lost. I hadn't experienced zero direction before. I didn't know what to do in Wrexham except hold out and wait to go to University. It felt like everything I'd prepared for had evaporated and for the first time, I truly didn't know what my next step was. It got worse. I went to University and dropped out after only one year. Even that path (being a decent academic) was denied to me. But when something is in you, it never truly dies. Four years later I was given the opportunity to volunteer as a full-time administrator for a conference charity. It's hardly social concern and it wasn't at all exciting but I knew I had to do it. I still don't know how I survived those first 6 months. I eventually became employed by the charity and worked with them for 3 years, honing event management skills and meeting extraordinarily inspirational people. I wasn't sure if the dream was being resurrected exactly and there was no clear path ahead of me, but I knew I was in the right place at the right time. But then our children came and I couldn't sustain an often 80hr working week and so I became a stay-at-home mum. Ouch! My identity felt completely stripped. Who was I anymore...the common cry of mothers everywhere? I never wanted a 9-5 life, a stay-at-home white picket fence, dog and 2 children kind of life but that is where I eventually found myself; well it was a brown fence and a cat who adopted us. In a way, although I totally adore my husband and children, I felt tied down – how do I travel the world and make contacts and spend months abroad with a family? My dream felt dead and stuffed, like some taxidermy animal to be glanced at in half wonder, half dismay.

Two years later a friend said that he knew of someone in a small, unheard of charity in Wrexham, looking for a part-time administrator, flexible hours. I initially said no. Then he asked again. I said no again, but later I made the phone call as we needed a bit more money and if I could work from home it would suit the kids. I started as the administrator and then became their donor relationship manager. Now I'm their overseas project coordinator managing programmes combatting poverty in Africa and Eastern Europe. Just 4 years into working with this charity, Teams4U, I've actively been part of making a difference in over 100,000 lives. In my journey I've had to watch close friends go out and fulfil what I felt to be my personal goals, as they, without any seeming direction or core life purpose, set up successful charities. It's hard watching others do what you can only dream of. But taking some financial risks and simply being who I am, I've found myself knocking on the door of my dream again."

As is evident in Ziz's story, the impact of not achieving even a simple dream can be devastating if we do not take hold of the situation and immediately do something to counteract the event. When we do not succeed at something we have aimed for, often the impact can affect our emotional world and it can stop us pressing on. When you look at many of the successful athletes, you find that significant injury has impacted them at some point in their career. At this point they could have given up on their dreams; those that have been successful have found a way to overcome. I know that when I have tried to lose a bit of weight, one single meal where I have eaten out and wanted to make sure I got value for money, can be enough to put me off track. I then continue eating more than I planned for the whole weekend.

There are many different things that can stop us from dreaming, including failed dreams. We need to address those things, and make changes to be able to start dreaming again and have a fulfilled life.

It's easy to think that if I have no dreams, then I cannot fail. The reality of this is that we are avoiding those feelings of failure but at the same time we are missing out on the joys of success. We all need to be able to make ourselves vulnerable to failure. This is where a great support team can be vital in fulfilling life goals. Top sports people have whole teams of people around them to help them back on track; they are the ones that keep faith in you even when you are unable to find that in yourself. As a church leader I see one of my roles is to help people believe in themselves and believe that they can live life to the full. If I talk to someone who is reluctant to dream I like to ask the necessary question, Why?

One of the reasons that people stop dreaming is that they have taken on a wrong identity. They may even have made incorrect statements about themselves consciously or unconsciously. If you believe that good things never happen to you or you are a failure at everything that you do then this will have an impact on everything you do. A simple illustration that demonstrates the point is that I do not like heights. Both consciously and subconsciously I avoid anything that involves heights. You will not find on my dream list things like undertaking a parachute jump, flying in a hot air balloon, or riding a roller coaster. Our internal voice, which will often have built up through our life experiences and by the things key carers have said to us, will act both as an encourager and a dream quasher. **The key question is how do we turn things around so we can enjoy life to the full?**

When we do the dream course I like to take people back to their childhood years and see if we can get them thinking firstly about positive and exciting childhood memories. We provide lots of different pictures to try and trigger some great memories. Alternatively, you could look at old photographs to remind you of special moments. When I look back like this I have a number of memories that stick in my mind. The memories make me smile. One of them is the family holidays down to Cornwall. In my mind this 2 week annual break was mainly sunny, it involved eating Cornish pasties, going to the beach for the afternoon and then getting back and buying an ice cream. It was a time of good memories. It made me realise that taking my wife back to Cornwall was something that I would like to do before too long; for me it would be a trip down memory lane which I am sure Sue will enjoy too, especially with a few cream teas. I realise it is a trip that is deeply important to me and is on my dreams list. Something that in many ways is easy to fulfil, it just needs a little planning.

The second part of this exercise is to look and see what we dreamed of becoming when we were growing up. Most people at this point realise that they did have dreams even if they have since been quashed.

Past failure

Past failure can be a significant blocker. It can create all sorts of emotions and pain. This can be exaggerated if the failure has in some way seemed public. Many people give up on dreams when they do not achieve the level they hoped in education. They give up future education and let dreams go. Society today is far better at offering alternative routes into different careers. Do you recognise this? Maybe it's time to take a second look at a career option that you believe is closed to you. Can you find a way of going back and getting the education that you need? I wonder how many people believe they cannot do maths but with the right help and support will realise that it is a subject within their reach.

Carrie's story which she calls "The Day after Failure" contains everything that would make you give up. Carrie is not someone who gives up. Here is a snippet of her story:

"I'd been struggling with a failing business for months. The moment of failure was crystalized when I had to ring my Aunt to ask for an advance on my inheritance from my Gran in order to avoid bankruptcy.

Three years earlier I was filled with confidence. I had a reputation as a successful business woman, so when I said I was going to start my own business everyone thought it was an obvious next step. I had a clear plan and a wealth of experience. I did all the right things. I even coached other people on how to set up their businesses.

By year three, I had more than enough work in the diary and everything was going to plan. Then, in the space of two weeks, all my clients cancelled the planned work because of budget pressures, my diary was empty, and not long after, so was my bank account.

For nine months I carried on, watching as all the businesses of those I had coached do all the things I was doing, but getting work where I wasn't. Eventually I had to admit defeat.

On the Monday morning I filled in the necessary paperwork to close the business down and made that phone call. I had failed and now everyone in my family knew it.

On the Tuesday, the day after failure, I got a phone call offering me work. Since then those phone calls have continued. I don't have a business website. I don't do any of the things you are supposed to do to be successful in business. I am recognised as an expert in my field and I get plenty of repeat business. This year, three years since I failed I will have earned a higher income than at any time in my life.

I am a very successful failed business woman."

Grief

Grief is something that can remove all of someone's life energy. It can be very difficult to walk through grief and depending on the nature of the loss can be months or years before you feel able to dream again. If you are in this situation I hope reading this will encourage you to pick up some of your old dreams as well as find some new ones.

Failure to complete a dream can be one source of grief. For other people they may have been through the sadness and difficulty of divorce and broken relationships and naturally feel very reluctant to start again. For others, grief is the result of a death of someone special. While we are not writing a book about dealing with grief and would recommend you finding the right support if you need it, we recognise that successful recovery involves dreaming again and finding a purpose in life. For someone who has been through divorce the thought of including a new life partner on their dream list might seem a step too far at this point. Maybe you can start by putting it down as your Everest dream and later when you have fulfilled

some Moderate, Challenging or Tough dreams you might
decide to re-categorise that dream and start to plan how you
can meet people again

Our words

We can also identify where we are at by our response to
others who are finding and pursuing life dreams. Are we
encouragers who believe anything is possible for them or are
we the one with the bucket of cold water waiting to dampen
down the other person's fire? Our words will reveal our heart.
If you find yourself looking for all the reasons why someone
else's dreams will not work and only seeing the barriers, then
you may well be doing the same for your own dreams.
Sometimes being aware of yourself and your responses to
others can be a pointer to opening up your own dreams.

Regret

Regret is another energy drainer. As with every feeling,
regret has its place in our lives as it helps us to review and
possibly do things differently in the future. There is a big
difference between this and making it our dwelling place.
There are regrets that can disempower you and reduce your
ability to dream or look to the future. If you are able to do
something about it then empower yourself by addressing the
regret and making changes. If you cannot, then find a way to
settle things in your mind so that you can move on
successfully. A missed dream, a missed moment, a missed
opportunity can be the catalyst for your future. The learning
experience can become an enabler.

Fear of Failure

There is one story in the bible that is often used to characterise failure. This is the moment that Jesus walks on water. When the disciples see Jesus they think that he is a ghost and they are very scared. I am sure we would all react in a similar way. When Jesus calls Peter to come to him, we find that Peter, despite the bad storm weather, is willing to get out of the boat and take a step. Even though he then looked at the wind and the large waves and began to sink, the fact he was willing to step out of the boat makes him a hero in my mind. I don't think I would have even been in the boat in the first place. Dreaming is a step towards the edge of the boat, enjoying life to the full and fulfilling what you are made for in the broadest sense. Living an extraordinary and interesting life, these are things found out on the walk!

Fear will limit you and may stop you. **Don't let a fear of failure become a barbed wire fence around your life.** We hope the processes detailed in this book will take you step by step and help you get through any fears. This is also where friends and fellow climbers can be a great asset. I know for me if I tell someone that I am going to do something I am much more likely to follow it through.

To Do:

Take a look at your dream list. Are there any things that you have left off the dream list because of your history? It might be the fear of someone's reaction, it might be past failure has become a block to your courage. Think again and add these to your list. Identify any blocks and make a note of them.

Take one of your dreams which you could easily walk by or leave out because of your history or fear. Make this dream one of your priorities. Overcoming is a key to fulfilled life.

Chapter 8 – Starting the Climb *(Nick Pengelly)*

"What does it take to live a life of adventure? The truth is, the first step is always the hardest, that's the one that takes the most courage. But I've learnt not to run from that fear and just do it". Bear Grylls – Ex SAS soldier, Adventurer, Writer, and Television Presenter.

"A journey of 1000 miles begins with a single step". Lao Tzu – Chinese philosopher.

Lights, Camera, Action – there is something a bit magical about those words as filming begins and another bit of the storyline is turned from script to a three dimensional reality. As a young child I remember being on holiday and walking up to a local post office to get my parents a newspaper. The place had been transformed to film the scenes for a TV drama. I watched as the producer helped set the scene with the support of the behind the scenes team and cast. Then that moment of Lights, Camera, Action came along with the clapperboard. The scene was simple with a young lad riding quickly to the post office dressed in clothes from a previous era. It was repeated a couple of times at different angles until the producer was happy and they moved on. After all the preparation, there has to be action.

Nikki never thought it was possible to live a fulfilled life. He described life as a living hell. His addictive personality had drawn him into a life of drugs and alcohol. This had resulted in him spending a significant time in prison. While in prison, Nikki would start to get life in order and truly believed he could be free. In many ways you could say this was not the life he had chosen but it was the one he had got ensnared in. It was a world that left him emotionally and physically bankrupt with little hope of escape. For Nikki at the time his impossible dream was to be free and wake up each morning without the cravings that were so hard to live with. Nikki was invited to join a 12 step program which would challenge everything in his life with the aim to help him turn life around. He described the program as beautiful but very difficult. The reality of the personal commitment needed means only a small portion of people are able to walk this road to freedom for any length of time. Nikki at this point was at his lowest and willing to do what it took to break the destructive pattern of life. A key part of success was having sponsors (mentors) who were not willing to give up. A number of years later if you met Nikki, you would not realise where he had come from but he will never forget as the reminder helps him stay clear of his previous addictions. He describes life as beyond his wildest dreams, forgiving himself for what he has done. He has found reconciliation with his family and children. He was able to walk his sister down the aisle at her wedding. He has fulfilled a dream of going up Mont Blanc and looks forward now to walking away from fear and the substances that had controlled his life. Nikki looks forward to new dreams that have now come onto his horizon, the possibility of running his own rehabilitation centre to help others become free.

With dreams it's not where you start, it's just vital that you do start.

We have spent a lot of time helping you identify your unclimbed mountains, provided you with a process to look at the more complicated ones and find a path of action to fulfilling these dreams. I am sure that along the way there are some dreams that you will have fulfilled before you have completed all the 'To Dos' at the end of each chapter. This is important as they give you some stories of success and help you realise that other dreams might also be possible. For some of you the process of turning a dream into a plan will have taken a lot of work and research; this in itself will have been part of the adventure. It will also have been a valuable process if you decided that something that you are pursuing as a dream does not really fit your life. I know I spent some time looking at the costs of setting up a holiday rental. At the beginning, it seemed a wonderful idea to have somewhere in one of my (emphasis on my, not our) favourite places. The more I looked not just at the costs but also the ongoing effort involved, the less attractive it seemed. In the end the idea did not seem at all attractive and would have cost a huge amount of money just to get established. I am also aware that while my preference is to visit familiar places, my wife loves to visit new places. This was one idea that has now been removed from my dream list; it was fun while the thought lasted. This process will allow you to clarify those dreams that will be worth pursuing and those that may not be.

After all this work in dreaming, finding fellow climbers to assist you in your climb, and then breaking the dream down into goals and sub goals, there is no point in having this plan of action and then not starting out.

Where to start?

We live quite close to the Snowdon mountain range in North Wales; it is an easy journey to go there for the day. At some point I would like to go to the top of Snowdon. I know that I will not make any of the difficult routes as I am not keen on heights. If I was to decide to go to the top I would need to select a starting point. There is one route that has grabbed my attention and is likely to be my starting point, it is a railway line that winds its way to the top of the mountain and stops at the café at the top. If I was going to take this route up and down the mountain I would need very different planning from any of the routes that require a day of genuine effort.

It is also important that when we are starting out on our life dreams that we can identity our starting point. This will partly be determined by the nature of our dream. If my dream is to stand on top of Snowdon, that is totally different to the dream of climbing to the top of Snowdon. The starting point for both trips will be a car park, but probably different car parks.

I remember speaking to some people who were dreaming of owning their own home. To them it seemed an impossibility because they knew the savings that they had were not sufficient and they had also read about the amount they could expect to borrow. We had ourselves just gone through a process of getting a mortgage which had initially seemed impossible as I had just started being self-employed. We encouraged the people involved to talk to the mortgage lender to find out the facts. The result of the whole journey was that they got their own house, the mortgage being much cheaper than the rent they were already paying.

In the last year we saw an opportunity to move house, having spoken to an advisor. The house was an important step for us to fulfil some of our life time dreams. We were living in a house on an estate but our dream was to live out in the countryside. A dream that many times had not happened due to practical and financial limitations. It was a dream that I could very easily have walked past because it seemed too difficult. I could have been writing this book and putting the house in the most challenging category. In fact each time we walked past the dream, this made the dream seem even more impossible. One advisor told us our dream was not possible, then another advisor made it sound easy but it turned out the advice we received was not particularly good. It's interesting that it was the bad advice that gave us the confidence to start the process. The initial part of getting the mortgage was also badly handled. Things happened so slowly that at one point we nearly lost the house we were trying to buy as the Vendors put the house back on the market. It was another turn in the road on what was already a challenging path. If I had been in the Vendors shoes I think I would have done the same. By this time I had the dream in my sights and was not ready to give it up. Even on the day of moving there were difficulties with the mortgage and we ended up moving in a few days later than planned. When I look back on the journey, the biggest challenge was actually getting started. It gave me the confidence when my daughter and her husband were looking to purchase a house and things were not coming together, to encourage them to keep going despite the odds. Just because you have a dream, even a dream you feel God has placed inside you does not mean the road is going to be straight. When the best laid plans are not working out it is important to review the dream and maybe even change the plan as Brian detailed in Chapter 5 with the acronym ACT. Sometimes circumstances change in terms of finance, family or even health. This might result in short or long term changes. We need to be able to embrace these changes to avoid giving up altogether.

Jane's story brings together many of the different stages that we have covered in the book. Like many people she longed to travel and do something of value. Enjoy reading her story:

"As a teenager I had an internal desire to go to Africa. Even when I saw something about Africa on the television I dreamed of going and having an impact. The dream had to go into the background as life moved on. I did not believe it was achievable and had no practical way of making it happen. When my children came along, the conflicting passions made me feel I would never go, it felt like a crushed dream. The more time moved on, the further away the dream became. I felt disappointed and felt I had missed it. I could not see how to create the opportunities."

For Jane, as with many people, it was sharing the dream that started to unlock it and open up the possibilities. There are always many people who will say that you cannot do something. It is important that you find people that say you can. A casual conversation in work turned what felt like an idle day dream into a possibility when some financial sponsorship was offered. There were still many hurdles to overcome but the process was strongly supported by Jane's husband, Kevin, who provided both the emotional and physical support with the family as he recognised the benefit to Jane of pursuing her dream.

> "It was not long after this that the ideal opportunity came up to work as a volunteer with Mercy Ships in Sierra Leone. The timing, the place, and the length of trip all came together."

During her trip, Jane was able to add value into the local community working in a Fistula clinic as well as at an Orthopaedic and Disability Hospital. In both places the fit was perfect with Jane's previous work experience. There was one extra dream that was unexpectedly fulfilled on this trip as Jane got the opportunity to experience and interact with a baby elephant at close quarters.

The long term positive benefits for Jane also show us how implementing and fulfilling important dreams are in our own lives. Jane said,

> "**I appreciate today even when today is tough. I find fulfilment in the little things.** When I remember what happened it helps me reignite future dreams and gives me the belief that I can see them happen."

To Do:

It's time to take some action. If you have not started then go back over the previous suggestions and get going. If you have worked through the book then take some time to get your action plan incorporated into daily life. Take time to investigate some options for some of your dreams. Chapter 9 provides a list of a few organisations that might be able to help you towards your dream. Tell people your stories and why not contact us. We would love to hear how you are getting on. Finally, get someone else on board with you to find their life dreams so they can share your journey.

Chapter 9 – Facilitating the Climb *(Nick Pengelly)*

We are aware that there is a vast quantity of information readily available on the internet for you to research when looking to start fulfilling your dreams. However, below are a few ideas of ours to help you on your way. These have all been checked by myself & Brian and we know them to be excellent in the service they provide and experts in their respective fields.

Financial Assistance/Advice

- Christians Against Poverty www.capuk.org

This award winning charity has a great history of helping people from all walks of life to get debt free as well as helping people develop the necessary skills to stay debt free. Even if you are not in debt their CAP Money Course can help you budget more effectively.

Charities

There are many excellent charities, some local, others national or international. Here are a few that we know to get you thinking and exploring the opportunities

- XL Mentoring www.xlm.org.uk

Involved with mentoring young people. Started in London but now moved to all over the UK.

- Teams4U – www.teams4U.com

Based in the UK, Teams4U was started by Dave Cooke to provide people who wanted to help vulnerable children and their families in Africa and Eastern Europe the opportunity to give more than just money.

- Kenya Children's Project www.thekcp.org

The KCP assist vulnerable and orphaned children in Kenya, as well as the communities that they are part of. They provide hope, practical love and a lasting legacy to those disadvantaged and unable to help themselves.

Charity Challenges

- Expedition Wise Ltd www.expeditionwise.com

Expedition Wise Ltd organise challenges and overseas expeditions for charities, companies and individuals. They focus on fantastic challenges with real quality and safety by running only a limited number per year. These include such challenges as Kilimanjaro, Everest Base Camp, London to Paris cycle, Coast to Coast cycle, Sahara Desert Trek, Iceland Volcano Trek and many more.

Climbing Unclimbed Mountains

- www.unclimbedmountains.com

They specialise in climbing previously unclimbed mountains in Nepal, so if you are literally looking to climb a new mountain and make a first ascent, check them out.

Chapter 10 – Continuing the Climb *(Brian Jackson)*

"If you dream it, you can do it." Walt Disney.

"Your dreams are always going to be the most important to you, so keep dreaming, keep believing, keep pressing forward. To all those warriors out there – be encouraged." Kai Greene, American IFBB professional bodybuilder, personal trainer, artist, and actor.

Whilst writing this book, both Nick and I have fulfilled quite a few of the dreams that were on our 'Dreams 21' lists and have had to continually update our lists. In fact, the writing of this book is a fulfilment of a dream of both of ours.

We all need to move forward to continue the climb, to reach more summits, to achieve more of our dreams. To illustrate this, we thought it would be a fitting ending to this book to share my latest Unclimbed Peak Expedition to Nepal that I made with a large group of participants and how it helped fulfil both my own and their individual dreams.

Here is our summit story:

"This was now my second time travelling to the Rolwaling Valley in Nepal, the epicentre of the 2ⁿᵈ large earthquake to hit Nepal in 2015. My previous expedition

to the valley had been in April of this year to climb an unclimbed peak called Omi Tso Go with a friend but this had been thwarted by a combination of bad weather and the route being too technical for us. As a result of the aborted attempt, we had some extra time on our hands and had used the time well recceing another unclimbed and unnamed peak on the Tibetan border. As with the tradition of naming peaks on the border in Tibetan, I "cautiously" named the peak Karbu Ri (White Peak) and hoped to come back with a group later in the year to attempt the first ascent of the mountain.

So here I found myself in Na, the last village along the Rolwaling valley, sitting with 12 members of my team (1 team member, Allan, had unfortunately already descended due to a very bad chest infection that was not improving). The next day, we headed off the beaten track, away from any tea houses and onto the start of the Rolwaling Glacier to camp at a place called Dudh Pokhari (4,700m/15,420ft), a yak herding area next to a beautiful holy lake. The walk to the lake was a step away from the standard trekking routes and the whole team were now using a main tent to eat in and even a small standing room only tent to use as a toilet with a hole dug in the ground – no more luxuries from here!

Two painful days of walking along the glacial moraine from Dudh Pokhari, and we eventually reached our High Camp or Advanced Base Camp (5,345m/17,536ft). Anyone who has walked for a long distance on a glacial moraine (solid ice covered with small and large boulders) *knows how mentally draining the rough terrain, constant attention to rock slippage, and the tedium of the same view as you just watch your feet, can be. On the occasions we did have to stop and look up over those two days, the view was a revelation of breathtakingly beautiful high Himalayan peaks, more than half of them unclimbed. We were walking into a cul-de-sac of mountains towards the border with Tibet.*

We set up High Camp right at the foot of the main ice fall of Karbu Ri, our intended peak. This allowed us to plot a route up through the ice fall to the snow slopes above that were heavily crossed in large crevasses. We were now down to 11 team members as Gary had to descend by helicopter from Base Camp (5,115m/16,781ft) due to a sudden onset of HACE (High Altitude Cerebral Edema).

Summit night, 1am, -20˚C (-4˚F), I sit up breathless in my tent with my tent buddie, Gwyn, as we start the awkward process of donning our layers of clothes whilst trying to remain in the confines of our sleeping bags so as not to lose any heat. Our daysacks are already packed with all manner of technical climbing gear and the obligatory electronics of any modern day expedition: camera, video, satellite tracker, satellite phone, GPS, and radios. For some inexplicable reason, my inner boots, that have been kept warm inside my sleeping bag, don't seem to want to go into my large outer boots and I take 15 minutes struggling to do this, becoming more and more out of breath in my growing frustration. All of the team have sorted themselves out in their teams and it is me who rolls into the mess tent last to check on everyone. All ready to go, we walk the 20 meters to the foot of the ice fall, put on our crampons and rope up to start the ascent. I have put people into 4 teams of mixed ability so that each team has a climbing Sherpa, a more experienced mountaineer and then a relatively less experienced mountaineer. On my rope, I have team member Tom Carrick and Munal Gurung. Within minutes of being on the glacier, I receive the news via my radio that Gwyn has had to go down as he has been ill for a few days and is drained of energy. This is terrible news and hits my confidence at this early point in the summit attempt and I walk on, head low, as I quietly reflect that this is now 3 of my team who will not have the chance of making the summit. My whole rationale for setting up this expedition is to allow people to stretch their limits and achieve more than they ever thought possible so I am bitterly disappointed that illness has robbed Allan, Gary and Gwyn of the opportunity to stand on an unclimbed mountain. High altitude mountaineering can be such a random and fickle affair when just a simple small cough can possibly end your chances of summiting; it never seems fair.

I need to rid myself of negative thoughts at this time and push on, so we do just that as a team and make amazing progress through the initial ice fall and onto the moraine before crossing back to the main snow slopes of the South Face. This is where our climbing Sherpas have laid out over 600m of fixed line to allow us to clip in safely through the heavily crevassed area as we climb up through a maze of adjoining snow slopes of 30 - 75°. I look back and can see a line of head torches as the other 3 rope teams are working their way up the ice fall and onto the South Face to join us. It is too cold to stop so we push on changing our gait from walking forwards to side stepping on the steeper sections to front pointing on the short near vertical sections, clipping our jumars to the fixed line when needed. We are soon on the final section of the South Face with only one steep ramp to climb to access the col (5,700m/18,701ft) between Langdung to our West and Karbu Ri, to our East. I am now getting excited as the more technical aspects of the climb (as we could perceive from down at High Camp) have now almost been completed and I start to see it as a real possibility that we can get the whole team to the summit. A final adrenaline rush of energy and I practically jog to the col to whoop with joy as I now stand directly on the border with one foot in Nepal and one foot in Tibet. Suddenly, the view of my feet and pool of light of my head torch is replaced with the wide open vista of the huge drop into Tibet and the outline of more and more fantastic mountains. We turn off our head torches and stop on the border for a while allowing our eyes to adjust as we can see the outline of the peak becoming clearer as the night slowly turns to day; the heavens lighten and dawn approaches with a mauve and pink sky. What a privilege to stand here on the Nepal/Tibet border and witness an amazing sunrise! The sun slowly peaks over the mountains as it crests the summit of Dragnag Ri and floods the whole area with warmth and light. With the daylight comes the whole panoramic view of the Himalayas laid out before me – wow!

Ahead lies the West Ridge which is a long slow plod on 30 degree snow slopes with some crevasses to cross before standing on the saddle between the south and north summit. From our walk in and camps, we have only been able to see the south summit above us so it is my first view of the higher north summit which rises much further into Tibet. I can see that the north peak seems to be split with a large crevasse just before the summit so it is time to keep walking on our rope and see how close we can get to the top. Another hour of walking brings our rope team to the final slope now heading due north to reach the summit. I now take over the lead as I want to film with no footprints in front of me showing the virgin territory we are covering. I am panting as I walk and we head closer and closer to the main summit when I come to the crevasse we saw from the saddle – it is deep, wide and sweeps across east to west cutting us off from the highest point. I stop and bring up the others. Munal, our climbing Sherpa thinks we can make it over by following it along to its narrowest point and crossing on a snow bridge. This of course means heading downhill on the very steep sloped side of the mountain to reach this point and it also means me continuing to lead to see how stable the snow is at the end of the visible part of the crevasse. I make it down and with a "keep the rope tight", I make my way across and over the crevasse to lead out the rope and then bring both Tom and Munal over. Only 20m now lays between us and a successful summit. I plod forward slowly, savouring the experience and reach the top with a yell and a holler – wahhooo! Tom and Munal quickly join me to celebrate and take in the view. It is only now that I realise we can see Everest and Cho Oyu and Lhotse and Shishapangma and many other peaks that are laid out before us.

We await the rest of the team and celebrate as each person reaches us and then take a reading on our satellite tracker – 6,010m/19,718ft (Lat: 27.954571, Long: 86.494203). Dawa Rita Sherpa hands me our prayer flags bought from the Bouddinath in Kathmandu and blessed at the Puja ceremony which I then fix to the peak with a snow thread. Our team of 10 climbers (Brian Jackson, Tom Carrick, Ben Brittain-Dodd, Tom Furey, Catherine Husted, Heather Bentley, Kieran Toner, Phil Absolon, Simon Wooller and Cat Cameron) and 4 Sherpas (Munal Gurung, Dawa Rita Sherpa, Mindu Sherpa, Mingma Dorje Sherpa) made the summit

Summit photos are taken with charity flags and after only the briefest time on what feels like the roof of the world, we start on down. An amazing first ascent in the Himalayas!"

To reach the summit with 14 people in total was amazing and fulfilled one of my dreams to reach the summit of a new mountain as a first ascent with a large group, but it was not just my dream being fulfilled. Here are the comments from some of those who took part in this Unclimbed Peak Expedition:

"I reached my goal of developing life-long friendships on this expedition." Gwyn Griffiths.

"I dreamed of completing a second unclimbed peak summit and the journey in was amazing but to reach the top of two

places where no one else has ever been – what more could you ask for?" Heather Bentley

"An incredible experience. I found it really emotional when I got to the top. I just can't believe it. I am so pleased with my achievement, but over and above that, I feel mentally stronger now and better equipped to face any challenges that life may throw at me. I suppose this sort of experience teaches self-reliance and self–belief and shows that no dreams are impossible if you work hard and put your mind to it." Phil Absolon

As Phil so aptly says, no dream is impossible if you work hard enough, so please keep dreaming and putting the hard work in to achieve them. Both Nick and I hope that this book has inspired you to do so and that you continue to dream and dream big.

Keep on Dreaming

Keep on Climbing your Unclimbed Mountains

References / Bibliography

Matthew Kelly - The Dream Manager - Hyperion Books

Leon Taylor - MENTOR: The Most Important Role You Were Never Trained For   - Soap Box Books

Bill Johnson - Dreaming with God - Destiny Image Publishers

John Kirkby - Nevertheless: The Incredible Story of One Man's Mission to change thousands of People's lives - CAP Books

Peter Drucker – People and Performance: The Best of Peter Drucker on Management

Ellen MacArthur - Race Against Time. - Penguin

James Cracknell and Ben Fogle - The Crossing: Conquering the Atlantic in the World's Toughest Rowing Race - Atlantic Books; Main edition

Kenneth Blanchard – The One Minute Manager – William Morrow and Company

Bear Grylls - Mud, Sweat and Tears - Channel 4

Lonely Planet's Ultimate Travel List: The 500 Best Places on the Planet...Ranked (Lonely Planet General Reference)   - Lonely Planet; 1 edition

Keith Foskett - The Last Englishman: A Thru-Hiking Adventure on the Pacific Crest Trail Kindle Edition

The Bible (New International Version)